THE **WIN-WIN** WORKPLACE

THE
WIN-WIN
WORKPLACE

HOW THRIVING EMPLOYEES
DRIVE BOTTOM-LINE SUCCESS

Angela Jackson

CEO of Future Forward Strategies

Berrett–Koehler Publishers, Inc.

Berrett-Koehler Publishers, Inc.
1333 Broadway, Suite P100
Oakland, CA 94612–1921
Tel: (510) 817–2277
Fax: (510) 817–2278
bkconnection.com

ORDERING INFORMATION

Quantity sales. Special discounts are available on quantity purchases by corporations, associations, and others. For details, please go to bkconnection.com to see our bulk discounts or contact bookorders@bkpub.com for more information.

Individual sales. Berrett-Koehler publications are available through most bookstores. They can also be ordered directly from Berrett-Koehler: Tel: (800) 929–2929; Fax: (802) 864–7626; bkconnection.com.

Orders for college textbook / course adoption use. Please contact Berrett-Koehler: Tel: (800) 929–2929; Fax: (802) 864–7626.

Distributed to the US trade and internationally by Penguin Random House Publisher Services. The authorized representative in the EU for product safety and compliance is EU Compliance Partner, Pärnu mnt. 139b-14, 11317 Tallinn, Estonia, www.eucompliancepartner.com, +372 5368 65 02

Berrett-Koehler and the BK logo are registered trademarks of Berrett-Koehler Publishers, Inc.

Printed in the United States of America

Berrett-Koehler books are printed on long-lasting acid-free paper. When it is available, we choose paper that has been manufactured by environmentally responsible processes. These may include using trees grown in sustainable forests, incorporating recycled paper, minimizing chlorine in bleaching, or recycling the energy produced at the paper mill.

Library of Congress Cataloging-in-Publication Data
Names: Jackson, Angela (Founder of Future Forward Strategies), author.
Title: The win-win workplace : how thriving employees drive bottom-line success / Angela Jackson. Description: First edition. | Oakland, CA : Berrett-Koehler Publishers, Inc., [2025] | Includes bibliographical references and index.
Identifiers: LCCN 2024036764 (print) | LCCN 2024036765 (ebook) | ISBN 9798890570543 (hardcover) | ISBN 9798890570550 (pdf) | ISBN 9798890570567 (epub)
Subjects: LCSH: Job satisfaction. | Employee morale. | Job enrichment.
Classification: LCC HF5549.5.J63 J325 2025 (print) | LCC HF5549.5.J63 (ebook) | DDC 650.1—dc23/eng/20240918
LC record available at https://lccn.loc.gov/2024036764
LC ebook record available at https://lccn.loc.gov/2024036765

First Edition

32 31 30 29 28 27 26 25   10 9 8 7 6 5 4 3

Book production: Westchester Publishing
Services Cover design: Ashley Ingram
Author photo: Rick Bern Photography

*To Fannie and George Lassiter who taught
me the value of a good day's work.*

And to Chris and Yuki for being the loves of my life.

Contents

Foreword by Jim McCann   ix

Introduction   A New World Order for Work   1

Chapter 1   Centering Employee Voices   21

Chapter 2   Committing to Win-Win Relationships   32

Chapter 3   The Whole Employee: How Intersectional Inclusion Unlocks Potential   52

Chapter 4   Reimagining Employee Benefits   69

Chapter 5   Activating Frontline Leaders   82

Chapter 6   Rethinking Credentials   104

Chapter 7   Developing Deep Talent Benches   122

Chapter 8   Using Human-Capital Reporting as a Competitive Strategy   137

Chapter 9   Distributing Leadership: Letting Every Worker Be an Entrepreneur   153

Chapter 10   How to Measure Impact and ROI in the Win-Win Workplace   170

Conclusion   Reaping the Rewards of a Win-Win Workplace   189

Discussion Guide   197

Appendix A: The Nine Win-Win Workplace Pillars   199

Appendix B: Facilitator Guide   205

Notes	211
Acknowledgments	223
Index	225
The Win-Win Workplace Toolkit	245
About the Author	247

Foreword

In the world of organizational psychology and leadership, few names resonate as strongly as Angela Jackson's. Her journey is marked by eloquence, intelligence, and a profound impact on those she encounters. My relationship with Angela began in a rather serendipitous manner during a Worth Media event at the time hosted by Juliet Scott-Croxford. It was there that I first witnessed Angela's remarkable presence. She was articulate, thoughtful, and undeniably brilliant.

Our paths crossed again when I had the opportunity to invite her to another event.

During our preparatory call, I found myself even more impressed by her depth and insight. Angela exceeded every expectation I had, and our professional relationship quickly evolved into a lasting connection.

Angela's credentials are nothing short of impressive. She is currently teaching at Harvard, runs her own consulting firm, and is an accomplished author. Her contributions to the field are invaluable, and the insights she's outlined in this book highlight the need for purpose, collaboration, and shared success in the workplace.

The insights and lessons presented in *The Win-Win Workplace* can be applied in many ways, both personally and professionally.

By reading this book, you will gain valuable knowledge and understanding that can help you navigate the changing landscape of work and find purpose, collaboration, and shared success. It offers actionable solutions for confronting biases and systemic barriers within corporate structures and provides a road map for creating a new kind of workplace where employees and companies can thrive together.

I believe that this book is an important and worthwhile investment of your time and thoughtfulness.

I highly recommend this book to anyone interested in creating a better future for work. It is a call to action for leaders at all levels who are ready to transcend the transactional status quo and build a "Win-Win workplace." I hope that you will find it as enlightening and thought-provoking as I have.

Angela Jackson is a force to be reckoned with, and I am honored to have her as a colleague and friend. Her journey is one of continuous growth and unwavering dedication, and I am excited to see the impact she will continue to make with this book and in the world of organizational psychology and beyond.

Jim McCann
Founder, CEO, and Chairman, 1-800-Flowers.com
Chairman, Worth Media

A NEW WORLD ORDER FOR WORK

Return-to-office revolt. The Great Resignation. Gig economy takeover. Quiet quitting. The signs of worker discontent are everywhere these days, and they all point to a radical transformation brewing in the global workplace as those of us who spend fully one-third of our lives working for a paycheck find ourselves, in the post-pandemic world, craving more. We want purpose, collaboration, and shared success. Yet, the current model of work often leaves us feeling disengaged, unfulfilled, and trapped in a cycle of "employee versus their employer."[1]

I'm here to prove to you that it doesn't have to be this way and to show you how successful organizations are already treating the self-inflicted wound that is the modern workplace.

This isn't the feel-good manifesto of a starry-eyed dreamer. This is the battle cry of a wounded soldier who lived the rat race, barely survived it, and then ventured into the trenches of academia, boardrooms, and countless conversations with leaders of the modern workforce to study and learn. I wanted to find the key to making work in the twenty-first century, even with the rise of AI robots, a real "Win-Win." And not just for the lucky few at the top who reap the benefits of a company's bottom line, but for the barista slinging lattes, the coder buried in algorithms, and the janitor keeping the lights on. For everyone.

SKIN IN THE GAME

I was flying high. By age thirty, I was the head of new channels marketing at Nokia, with business school education that the company paid for and more frequent-flyer miles—Executive Platinum on American, Premier 1K on United—than I could ever use. I was paid good money (more than enough to pay for my own master's degree) to sell the latest Nokia mobile device into retail and was a regular business traveler at the Four Seasons in Beverly Hills and the Mandarin Oriental in Singapore, sometimes in the same week. I was crushing the whole upwardly mobile thing.

Until I came crashing down.

It was a typically insane business trip in October 2007. I arrived in Los Angeles from New York on a Monday night with just enough time to sleep, dazzle at my Tuesday 8 a.m. client meeting, and then, with peak efficiency, catch my early afternoon flight to New York and then Helsinki, Finland. Driving through L.A. that morning, I remember thinking, *I hope they don't have a lot of questions for me because I need to make that flight.* I saw the sign for my turn too late. I didn't see the oncoming car at all. I injured my neck and back and dislocated my shoulder. My body was one big bruise. The pain was excruciating. Throughout six months of intensive physical therapy so that I could use my left arm again, I thought about all the other signs I hadn't seen as I barreled toward so-called success. The empty apartment I was never in. The family I never saw. I couldn't remember the last time something real—something other than an expensive new designer bag or the latest New York restaurant—brought me real joy. *What's the point of all this? Am I here just to make more money for the company and, for myself, just to buy more things? There must be a better way to work, a better way to live.* I had a lot of time to think.

"Pivot" is a word we hear more and more in the global discussion of work. Well, I pivoted. Hard. I went back to school for a doctorate in education leadership, focusing my research on organization and system change, and then went out into the world to see how different workplaces worked in real life. Interviewing hundreds of workers, I made it my job to understand what they need from their employers and what barriers they face to getting what they need. Then I sought out employers who were already on the road to creating that mythical *better way to work* so many of us crave.

The questions swirling around my search—about the human part of human resources; about how to attract, hold on to and build talent; about how to invest in employees as people so that they, in turn, feel invested in their work—were first stirred in childhood, in the shadow of the shuttered Chrysler factory in Kenosha, Wisconsin. From the time I was four, when my mother died, I was raised by my grandparents, neither of whom had more than a sixth-grade education. My grandfather was proud to be a Chrysler man and union member, making $7.25 an hour on the Kenosha plant's assembly line, installing doors on Chrysler Reliant and Plymouth Sundance cars. His pay was well over minimum wage at the time, and it afforded him good healthcare, job security, a pension, and a sense of community. Until it didn't.

I was thirteen when that factory closed, laying off 5,500 workers, including my grandfather, who was then sixty-four years old.[2] Our neighbor across the street lost his job, so did my uncle. It felt like the whole town was suddenly out of work.[3] Generations of workers kept the Kenosha plant humming for more than a century, and Chrysler, one of our community's last remaining employers paying blue-collar workers a family-sustaining wage, was now gone.

Chrysler had trained my grandfather to do just one thing—and to do it expertly. When that job disappeared, Chrysler had nothing more to offer him. He, like hundreds of others in my community, was left with no ability to pivot, no skills for transitioning to other work. The plant and its managers were transactional—you give us labor; we give you wages—and made no lasting investments in their people or community. That's a broken system, and one that lives on, even though rapidly advancing technology and worker discontent makes this system ultimately unsustainable.

FROM BREAKING TO WINNING

I have lived experience with the devastation—to my working-class grandparents and our community, to my totaled rental car and battered body—of the broken system of work. But it's much more than personal. And it's more than an American phenomenon. My postdoctoral exploration of workforce investments and the future of work was a deep dive into more than 1,200 companies and organizations around the world, from Walmart, the largest employer in the world, to Jergens Inc., a small manufacturing company, and TÜV SÜD, a global company that provides safety testing and certification for products we touch in our daily lives, including children's toys, car parts, and medical devices. This research involved extensive interviews and data collection over more than six years, a period that included perhaps the most disruptive force ever to hit the global workplace, the 2020–2021 COVID-19 pandemic. The findings confirmed my suspicions: the status quo of workplaces was choking the life out of both people and profits. But amid the wreckage, I also found glimmers of hope: organizations defying the old unworkable status quo model by creating for their people—leaders, managers, and workers alike—oases of collaboration, trust, and shared success. That's what I call a Win-Win workplace.

How can you get there, too? In the next phase of my research, I pulled together the sometimes one-off initiatives I encountered in various organizations and then analyzed them against theories that my fellow organizational change and MBA nerds will appreciate: human capital theory, stakeholder theory, systems thinking, social exchange theory, equity theory, and distributed leadership. From there, I devised a holistic approach to rewiring the transactional status quo workplace to a Win-Win workplace: By prioritizing employee well-being, creating an environment where everyone has a fair chance to succeed regardless of background or identity, fostering continuous learning and development, and managing human resources strategically, organizations can be adaptive, inclusive, and financially sustainable through whatever the future holds for us all.

The Win-Win Workplace: How Thriving Employees Drive Bottom-Line Success confronts biases and systemic barriers within corporate structures, offering actionable solutions for recruiting practices, performance management, and more. It's a call to action for leaders—C-suite, management, and worker-bee leaders alike—who are ready to transcend the transactional status quo and build a new kind of workplace—a Win-Win workplace—where employees and companies can thrive together. Is this an easy path? No. But imagine the rewards. Imagine a workplace where

- employees feel valued, empowered, and connected to a purpose greater than company profits;
- companies flourish through innovation, collaboration, and peak performance; and
- we, as a society, collectively move beyond the win-lose mentality and create a world of shared success.

THE ZERO-SUM WORKPLACE ISN'T WORKING

During my research, I focused on companies across sectors who were doing well and where their employees were thriving while others who were set in their ways were falling behind. I found two opposing strategies at play. One valued the old ways of work, where there must be losers so that the winner can take all the riches. I call this the Zero-Sum workplace. It's often based on seniority and hierarchies, where years of service and your perch on the "org chart" mean more than performance and potential. A Zero-Sum workplace is one that doesn't prioritize employee well-being or consider employees' lives outside of work, even for those at the top.

Globally, 40 percent of workers say they grapple with an inadequate work-life balance.[4] Within this group, a staggering 67 percent blame things intrinsic to their work—like unclear expectations—and/or their workplace culture, like pressure to work extra hours and be constantly available, all while feeling undervalued.[5] A Zero-Sum workplace often neglects continuous learning and development and falls short when managing human resources strategically. As an example, the Anne E. Casey and Joyce Foundations found that most corporations spend 80 percent of their professional development dollars on their highest wage earners, with the remaining dollars used for safety training for the rest—mainly entry-level workers and frontline employees.[6] This especially resonated with me. My employer paid for my graduate program at a time when I had the resources to get it myself. Lower-level employees got little to no help climbing their career ladders. In this sort of Zero-Sum workplace, the privileged get more privileges and perks. The rest? They get safety training. It's like telling the commoners, *Just get your job done without bleeding all over the place.*

Whether it is a lack of imagination or the inertia of historical practices, these companies hold their employees at a distance by design, treating them as disposable and replaceable, thinking that will help leadership make "tough" decisions in the long term. These are places where regular turnovers and layoffs (rebranded with the gentler sounding "reduction in force" or "RIF") are the gold standard to winning the competitive advantage. We've seen it a lot recently: one tech company will have a RIF, and others will follow suit. As Jeff Shulman, a professor at the University of Washington's Foster School of Business says, "There is a herding effect in tech. . . . The layoffs seem to be helping their stock prices, so these companies see no reason to stop. They're getting away with it because everybody is doing it. Workers are more comfortable with it; stock investors are appreciating it."[7]

The Win-Win Workplace isn't a eulogy for this broken workplace. Anyone can rattle off what's wrong with work. Frankly, that's depressing. Instead, this book focuses on what's going right. Armed with data, real-world stories, and a road map that's been test-driven in real companies, I'm here to show you how to tear down the walls between leaders, managers, and frontline workers and implement a strategy whereby workers thrive and your business succeeds. I will highlight companies across healthcare, transportation, tech, manufacturing, and financial services that are choosing a different strategy, a new playbook. In contrast with the Zero-Sum workplace, these companies

- position a purpose greater than profits front and center of the organization's raison d'être (for a medical device company, the purpose can be innovation to improve quality of life for people with disabilities; for a toy manufacturer, purpose can be bringing joy to young and old);
- prioritize all employees' well-being;
- embrace and celebrate diversity and inclusion;
- build a community that values the unique contributions and perspectives of every individual;

- foster continuous learning and development;
- manage human resources strategically; and
- regularly communicate progress at all levels to ensure transparency and buy-in.

THE MAKING OF A ROAD MAP: FROM WORKER SKILLS TO WORKER WELL-BEING

Here's where I want you to know exactly (but briefly) how the Win-Win workplace strategy developed, so that you can feel confident it's deeply rooted in real data. My research began in 2018 at New Profit, a national nonprofit with a twenty-year history of investing in entrepreneurs and organizations committed to breaking down barriers between people and their opportunity. Its Future of Work Grand Challenge aimed to prepare more than 10 million low-wage workers for career success by 2025.[8] With a multimillion-dollar purse, New Profit's idea was to give a "moonshot" prize to innovators who were developing products and services to help workers gain the tech skills that would be in demand in the future—such as cloud computing, cybersecurity, and climate mitigation. My job was to conduct a qualitative analysis of the 1,200-plus organizations that applied for the prize. To do this, I collected the details of their training ideas and solutions, as well as the demographics of their leadership and self-reported human capital. We used the same metrics to document the progress of New Profit's ultimate investments in prizewinners.

My New Profit colleagues and I went into this thinking that skills were the answer—that what the future workplace needed were investments *now* in technological solutions for giving low-wage workers the skills they would need to succeed moving forward. We conducted in-depth interviews with over a hundred corporate executives across multiple sectors and industries. These included oil and gas extraction, and the manufacturing of cars, machinery, electronics, and food products. Our interviews also went deep into service industries, including transportation, warehousing, finance, insurance, information technology, communication, education, healthcare, hospitality, and professional and business services (consulting). From these same industries, we interviewed 80 employers and 180 workers. For even broader perspective on what a future workplace—and future worker—needs, we interviewed 75 workforce intermediaries, including United Way, Chamber of Commerce, and the Society for Human Resource Management; and 150 founders of startup innovating in the fields of future of work, talent management, and generative AI, including leaders from Microsoft, Workday, and SkyHive. Additionally, we created a worker advisory board of 200 workers who were representatives of the United States to gain insights from various leadership perspectives.

Two months into this research, I began to suspect that upskilling workers would not be the silver bullet we imagined. And so, I convened three summits—in Detroit (October 2019) Boston (January 2020), and Los Angeles (March 2020)—bringing together employers, worker-training startup founders, MIT researchers, human resources experts, and frontline workers. These workers included everyone from McDonald's cashiers and fry cooks to JPMorgan Chase bank tellers, techs at Slack, and nurses at hospitals. We held "design sessions" where together these groups with a 360-degree view of the workplace imagined what skills workers would need for sustainable careers that could support them (and their families) into the future. Lo and behold, we kept hearing not just about skill gaps, but about other barriers that played an even bigger role in holding workers back. Things like access to childcare and transportation. At the January convening, one state official surprised me by saying, it's not hard for people to get a job. The challenge is when life happens like their car breaks down or their kid must stay home sick from school. It was becoming clear that the future of work needed more than advanced worker skills. It needed innovations around our human capital processes—and simple employee well-being.

THE RESEARCH SHIFT: THE FUTURE OF WORK BECOMES THE PRESENT

When COVID-19 was declared a pandemic in March 2020, I saw the future of work become the present. Overnight, people in industries like travel and restaurants needed to make immediate career transitions while millions of others were suddenly figuring out how to teach school or conduct doctors' visits remotely from home offices. It became clear that there were two classes of workers: those who could afford to shelter in place, earn, learn, and thrive; and a second-class majority who had to settle for low wages and poor benefits while being routinely exposed to the virus. Our research at New Profit took on a greater urgency and expanded to address workers displaced by the pandemic and the automation that accompanied remote work. Because while 2020 was abnormal, crises are not. And when wars arise in other nations, or economic depressions or natural disasters hit ours, workers without basic supports in place stand to lose a lot. Maybe everything.[9]

By the end of the New Profit Future of Work Grand Challenge in 2022, I had spoken to hundreds of workers, scores of employers, and the organizations that support them. These conversations— and the data and document sharing that followed—made me realize that employees would not be able to "skill their way" to better outcomes in the future of work. The workplaces themselves needed a radical transformation where employers take on a greater responsibility for the holistic well-being of their employees. That's the way organizations thrive in the future of work—*alongside* their thriving workers. Next, I needed to see what employee well-being would mean to an organization's bottom line.

CONCEPTUALIZING A WIN-WIN WORKPLACE

I left New Profit in 2022 and founded Future Forward Strategies, a labor-market analytics and strategies firm. This enabled me to focus my research on basic supports for workers, and to see if there was an economic case to be made for a business strategy of innovations around human capital and employee well-being. Was there a better approach to human capital management—something more holistic than one-off initiatives like Summer Fridays—that could lead to better business sustainability?

My team and I took a deeper, broader look at the 1,200-plus companies from my New Profit research. From this analysis, I identified nine practices of what I had begun to conceptualize as "Win-Win workplaces." I call these practices the nine pillars of the Win-Win workplace, and they are central to creating sustainable and human-centered organizations. The nine pillars, which are summarized below, systematically address high turnover, absenteeism, reduced productivity, and poor customer service—all critical issues of the Zero-Sum workplace that have worsened since the pandemic.

Pillar One: Centering Employee Voices

- Shift from suggestion boxes to actionable feedback mechanisms.
- Ensure that employee concerns and ideas are represented in all areas of the business, and that employees see their feedback in action, contributing to positive change.
- See positive correlations for profits, revenue, stock price, and asset valuation.
- *Bottom line: When employees see their ideas used to make positive changes, they feel more involved in the company's success and are more likely to stay (lower turnover).*

Pillar Two: Cultivating Mutualistic Working Relationships

- Build and nurture positive, collaborative Win-Win relationships between employees and employers.
- Expand the notion of employee rewards beyond salary and wages to include purpose and an alignment of values so that employees feel they are contributing more than the simple completion of tasks.
- *Bottom line: When employees feel appreciated and contributory, the result for the company is higher profits, higher asset valuation, and lower turnover, which means lower costs over the long term.*

Pillar Three: Implementing Intersectional Inclusion Strategies

- Create a workplace where employees can show up authentically without feeling they have to mask their identity, background, or any personal challenges.
- Acknowledge and value the unique experiences of employees from diverse backgrounds.
- Move beyond benefits designed for a single demographic.
- Create a work environment that leverages and celebrates the identities of all employees.
- *Bottom line: When employees feel comfortable bringing their whole selves to work, it can redirect energy spent hiding issues to creating value for the company, leading to higher profits and higher asset valuation.*

Pillar Four: Reimagining Employee Benefits

- Offer a variety of benefit options to meet individual employee needs.
- Move beyond traditional benefits to include options like caregiving services and work-life coaching.
- Allow employees to recommend benefits that work for them.

- *Bottom line: Giving employees ownership over their benefits increases satisfaction and loyalty, which can actually boost all areas of the company's finances—profits, sales, stock price, and overall value.*

Pillar Five: Activating Frontline Leaders

- Empower frontline leaders to champion inclusion efforts.
- Empower frontline managers to design and implement human-centered strategies.
- Move decision-making closer to the work being done.
- Increase employee ownership and accountability.
- *Bottom line: Makes employees feel more responsible (ownership) and invested (engagement), leading to higher profits and a more valuable company (higher asset valuation), plus lower turnover.*

Pillar Six: Hiring STARs versus Prioritizing Credentials

- Hire based on a candidate's skills, talents, abilities, and results (STARs) rather than solely on traditional academic/educational credentials.
- Develop innovative assessment methods to identify talent through alternative routes.
- Expand the talent pool by considering candidates with diverse backgrounds and experiences.
- *Bottom line: Opens the door to a wider range of talented people who might not have a traditional education. This approach can lead to higher profits, higher asset valuation, and a potential boost in stock price.*

Pillar Seven: Developing Deep Talent Benches

- Nurture and grow talent within the organization to fill future leadership roles.

- Invest in training and development programs to grow internal talent.
- Retain top talent by offering career advancement pathways.
- *Bottom line: Keeping the best employees (retention of top talent) helps companies create a culture where everyone is always learning and improving (culture of learning and growth). This can earn the company a higher asset valuation.*

Pillar Eight: Using Human-Capital Reporting as a Competitive Strategy

- Use data and metrics related to employees (human capital) to inform strategic decision-making and then communicate the decision-making factors to employees.
- Track and measure human-capital data like employee compensation, training, and well-being.
- Increase transparency by disclosing relevant human-capital data.
- *Bottom line: Data-driven decision-making, improved workforce planning, and increased employee trust can lead to higher profits, more sales (revenue), and higher asset valuation.*

Pillar Nine: Distributing Leadership via Entrepreneurial Structures

- Move beyond rigid hierarchies toward flatter organizational structures.
- Empower employees at all levels within the organization to share ideas, expertise, and to take ownership and make decisions.
- Create a work environment where collaboration and innovation thrive.
- *Bottom line: Collaboration and innovation lead to increased agility and problem-solving capabilities. These can boost all*

areas of the company's finances—higher profits, more sales, increased stock price, and higher asset valuation.

Once we identified these pillars, we sought to understand how they impact financial performance. We investigated the connection between how closely businesses hewed to the Win-Win workplace pillars and how well they did financially over two years, looking at things like stock price, profits compared to total sales, and overall sales growth. We thought focusing on shareholder value was important because it reflects expectations of a company's future profitability. We suspected that investing in employees and creating better work environments would pay off in the long run, especially as experienced workers move into higher-level jobs. But we looked at all three financial measures to make sure our evidence was strong.

To understand how well companies followed the pillars, we looked at what they said in public reports and tax documents; we talked to both employers and employees; and we scoured websites like LinkedIn and Glassdoor for information on employee sentiment. We created a big data set of promises and certifications related to the nine pillars, scored each company's performance, and then did a regression analysis to see how the companies' use of them affected their financial performance.

To double- and then triple-check our findings, we partnered with JUST Capital and Burning Glass Institute, both research nonprofits, to run the same regression analysis on their own survey data sets. While their surveys didn't address all nine of our Win-Win workplace pillars, they overlapped enough—JUST Capital surveyed 950 corporations on social responsibility; Burning Glass, as part of their American Opportunity Index and other proprietary databases, had career histories and compensation data for almost 5 million US workers at 355 Fortune 500 companies—to be meaningful.

A striking 96 percent of our analyses showed a positive correlation between increased revenue or profit and the employment practices in our nine pillars. This is the empirical evidence baked into the new world order of *The Win-Win Workplace.*

KEY FINDINGS

1. Employers that center their employee voices are much more likely to retain their employees—and achieve significantly higher revenues.

2. Workplaces where employees have clear pathways to internal advancement achieve much better profits and valuation than those without such pathways.

3. Companies where employees have stock ownership plans achieve much higher revenues and assets.

4. Workplaces where employee benefits go beyond the traditional—to include offerings such as backup dependent care, paternity leave, and subsidized childcare—are more likely to achieve higher profits and valuation.

This book is your road map to achieving this vision, whether you're a CEO, C-suite leader, small business owner, or an employee trying to get ahead. We'll explore the urgent need for transformation, the limitations of the transactional model and the Zero-Sum workplace, and the core principles of building a Win-Win workplace. We'll delve into practical strategies, leadership mindsets, and the inevitable challenges you'll encounter along the way—all of it showcased in vivid (and, I hope, lively!) case studies.

The case studies that you will find in each chapter are the real stories of real people in real organizations—in the United States and overseas—that I encountered and studied in my research. This research included not only the extensive data collection and analysis previously described, but also one-on-one interviews with business leaders and workers alike. In Chapter Five, the second case study, titled "Global People Leaders," is presented as a composite of three organizations from my research that, for competitive and proprietary reasons, did not want to be identified.

PUTTING THE PILLARS IN PLACE

Think of the Win-Win workplace pillars as spokes on a wheel of fortune that you can spin for one pillar at a time and then repeat for the next pillar, depending on your workplace's needs. This cyclical Win-Win process of change ensures continuous improvement and adaptation within the workplace transformation journey.

*Six Steps to Launching
the Win-Win Process of Change*

Prepare

1. **Start by centering employee voices:** Consider employees' lived experiences and expertise and integrate their input and feedback to ground business decisions. Talk to people on the front line. Pay specific attention to frontline managers and include their analysis of any challenges and solutions.

Act

2. **Select which of pillars two through nine to work on next based on your workplace needs:** Be guided by employee-identified needs and pain points.

Refine

3. **Empower employees to develop new approaches to the selected pillar:** Go beyond feedback boxes by giving employees

voice and decision rights in shaping new solutions to issues that matter most to them and impact their work.

4. **Evaluate outcomes and adoption of the new approaches:** Gather feedback from employees on the effectiveness of the new approaches.

5. **Adjust the new approaches as needed:** Collaborate with employees to refine and amplify the impact of the new approaches.

Communicate and Learn

6. **Transparent communication:** Share updates on the implementation progress, the results of the changes, and key learnings from the actions. This communication should be clear, concise, and accessible to all employees.

Continue the cycle by repeating steps two through six for the next pillar. Center employee voices again when selecting the next pillar to address and in developing and implementing new approaches to that pillar. See Figure 1 which represents the Win-Win process of change diagrammatically.

In Chapter One, "Centering Employee Voices," we consider employee voice, whereby employees have a say in issues that matter most to them, and employee engagement, whereby employees become thought partners in all aspects of the business. We explore operationalizing employee feedback and participation in decision-making processes. This chapter provides a through line to each subsequent strategy, because without the centering of employee voices, the rest are just actions with no anchor.

Chapter Two, "Committing to Win-Win Relationships," lays out the pitfalls of the Zero-Sum workplace and challenges us to reimagine the employer-employee relationship and a workplace culture that values mutuality, well-being and aligns with personal values.

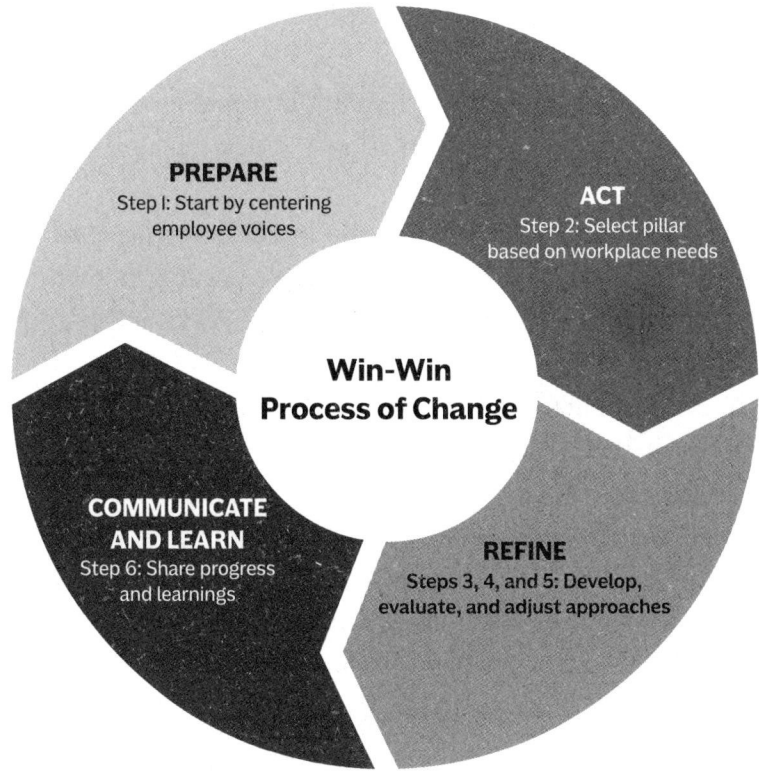

Figure 1. Win-Win Process of Change

In Chapter Three, "The Whole Employee," we address an element of inclusivity that is oft overlooked in the workplace and look at policies and practices that honor the multifaceted identities of employees.

Chapter Four, "Reimagining Employee Benefits," explores the importance of flexible benefits options that prioritize employee choice and autonomy.

In Chapter Five, "Activating Frontline Leaders," we delve into the complexities of maximizing middle-management leadership, offering strategies for meaningful organizational change.

Chapter Six, "Rethinking Credentials," challenges the notion of traditional credentials—pedigree and diploma—as the sole measure of talent, advocating for skills-based hiring and inclusivity in talent acquisition.

Moving forward, Chapter Seven, "Developing Deep Talent Benches," focuses on talent retention and development strategies for long-term growth.

In Chapter Eight, "Using Human-Capital Reporting as a Competitive Strategy," we explore how transparency in reporting human capital metrics can enhance accountability and organizational success.

In Chapter Nine, "Distributing Leadership," I advocate for flatter organizational structures that empower workers and foster collaboration and innovation.

Finally, in Chapter Ten, "How to Measure Impact and ROI in the Win-Win Workplace," we offer an approach to measuring the return on investment of implementing our nine pillars.

So, whether you're ready to dive in headfirst or prefer to take a more measured approach, the Win-Win workplace revolution awaits. Join us as we embark on this journey together, redefining the future of work one chapter at a time. Welcome—to a world where success is measured not only in profits, but also in building a workplace where everyone, from the CEO to the intern, can truly win. If you're ready to join the ranks of those who dare to dream of a better world of work, turn the page, and let's begin!

CENTERING EMPLOYEE VOICES

For too long, too many workplaces have thought of employees as an input: insert workers and out come product and profits. A Win-Win workplace treats employees as investments: treat employees well and reap bigger profits. It's a simple shift, but a radical one. It starts with centering employee voices, eliciting their perspectives, and factoring their concerns and ideas into company decision-making. This is the central pillar of the Win-Win workplace, from which all improvements emerge.

Large firms spend thousands of dollars a year for every companywide survey that they administer. In fact, some of the largest corporations have entire teams dedicated to "people analytics," collecting massive amounts of data that, in theory, should help these organizations improve employee satisfaction and reduce turnover. Indeed, employers are gathering more feedback from their workers than ever—whether through a vintage suggestion box in the employee lunchroom, 360-degree reviews (comprehensive individual performance evaluations by supervisors, peers, and subordinates), or Net Promoter Score, which is a measure of customer loyalty and satisfaction. So, the really vexing question is: With so much employee feedback being gathered, why are they still not

WHAT THE RESEARCH SAYS

My research found that organizations who actively listen to their employees—and then incorporate employee feedback into business and management decisions and give consideration in these decisions to the lived daily realities of their employees—tend to perform significantly better financially than their peers with Zero-Sum workplaces, where employee input is not sought, and workers are treated like replaceable machine parts. Analyzing data from 355 firms among the Fortune 500, I found that employee-centered companies who have invested in Win-Win workplaces have more valuable assets (39 percent), 44 percent had higher profits, and 38 percent had increased revenue. Furthermore, those organizations who focus on retaining employees experience additional advantages. They generate more revenue per employee and have a higher valuation in relation to their revenue. These findings underscore the critical role that employee voices and feedback can play in driving gains in financial performance, organizational value, and market standing.

feeling heard? Workers in 2024 were the most unhappy they've been since they were in the throes of pandemic shutdowns.[1] And employee satisfaction with their employers is among the lowest rates on record. A 2022 Gallup poll revealed that 76 percent of workers believe that their bosses don't care about their well-being.[2] That's the transactional model of the Zero-Sum workplace rearing its head. Our goal in a Win-Win workplace is to do more than gather employee feedback. We want to *take action* with that feedback, giving workers a real voice and tangible influence over the workplace conditions that are most important to them. Our goal is to foster healthier companies—more equitable, sustainable, and profitable companies.

Any strategy for creating a Win-Win workplace, if it is to be effective, requires employers to analyze their business's value chain and ensure that the whole employee—their feedback, their input, their lived experience and realities *plus* the business expertise they've accrued from their frontline jobs—is represented in all areas of the value chain. To help do this, there is an emergent specialty within data science called people analytics. The work that firms are undertaking with generative artificial intelligence (AI) to make sense of their data promises vital insights into developing smart solutions and programming that better serve both employees and the organizational bottom line. Throughout this book, I will offer ideas on how to leverage this technology in the building of our Win-Win workplace pillars.

I am *not* saying that everything employees assert in feedback must be followed to the letter. What I *am* saying is that it's essential to acknowledge workers at all levels as valuable sources of critical data, insights on innovation, and opportunities for efficiency. Their experiences at work *and* outside of the workplace can impact the bottom line. In 2024, research from Gallup found a connection between strong employee engagement and positive business results. These results include a 23 percent increase in profitability, 18 percent increase in productivity, 10 percent increase in customer loyalty and engagement, and reduced turnover.[3] It's a simple Win-Win: when employees are engaged, they help their businesses thrive.

No one is more passionately certain of this than Pete Stavros, an innovator in business organization who has proven the efficacy of centering employee voices (pillar one of the Win-Win workplace) at a little-known garage door manufacturer in Arthur, Illinois.

Case Study: *KKR: Opening Doors, Winning Hearts*

Kohlberg Kravis Roberts & Co. Inc., also known as KKR, is a powerhouse in the global financial world, investing in what they see as undervalued businesses, energy projects, and real estate to help them grow and succeed. When Pete Stavros took charge of the Industrials group within KKR in 2005, he began experimenting with ways to address a common problem impacting companies: strained employer-employee relationships that led to inefficient deliveries, waste, and low productivity. As the son of a Chicago construction worker who raised his family on a $15 hourly wage, Pete grew up knowing only one kind of worker-boss relationship: one of conflict. His dad and his coworkers seemed constantly at odds with their boss. Especially over hours. They were being asked to work during unpaid lunch breaks and would see their hours cut without explanation. "If you make fifteen bucks an hour, all you want are more hours and ideally some overtime. But the employer wants exactly the opposite," Pete shared.[4] "There were nonstop fights over hours that led to bad behavior and strikes that my family had to live through. My dad would say, 'I should care about quality, cost, and doing the job right and on time. But I don't.'" Pete remembered stories of worker retaliation like slow-walking their tasks, holding their tongues when they saw cost-saving opportunities, and intentionally disrupting operations by scheduling deliveries when no one would be available to receive them. It was even worse than a Zero-Sum arrangement, with each side taking steps to actually damage the other. Years later, these stories from his childhood fed Pete's determination at KKR to improve worker conditions—especially in blue-collar industrial jobs—by understanding the link between employee engagement and business outcomes.

When KKR bought C.H.I. Overhead Doors, a garage-door manufacturer in Arthur, Illinois, in 2015, Pete saw the potential for increased summer productivity, reduced waste, and enhanced safety at C.H.I., all of which could be controlled by employees. Pete also saw an opportunity to test a new employee engagement strategy he had begun experimenting with a few years earlier.

First, he and C.H.I.'s management undertook an initial employee survey (step one of the Win-Win process of change: identify opportunities to center employee voice). Only 30 percent of the workers participated in the survey—the first sign of the significant challenges C.H.I. faced. Those employees who did respond indicated that morale was low, and they had no faith that the survey would change anything about how they experienced working at C.H.I. They had seen ownership of C.H.I. change hands among private-equity firms four times in thirteen years and had learned to expect business as usual. They had heard empty promises before—about making the company a better, safer place to work—and injuries remained common, with 14 percent of employees sustaining reportable injuries each year.

Pete understood right away that KKR and C.H.I. management would need to take bold steps to change the workers' minds and ensure that worker incentives were aligned with worker goals. He along with C.H.I.'s management got to work implementing his employee-engagement experiment: the company would make every employee into an owner and financial stakeholder, promising a slice of profits with a minimum payout of $15,000 if the company achieved its targets upon sale. KKR and C.H.I. management were transparent with the workforce and communicated clearly (pillar eight of the Win-Win workplace) that their goal was to sell the company at a profit in five to seven years. The premise, as KKR had successfully tested at other firms, was that if employees felt and were treated like owners, they would be more invested in the company's success and more likely to suggest improvements and manage resources responsibly.

Convincing the employees that management's profit-sharing offer was legitimate proved challenging though, considering the deep-seated distrust and resentment that had built up over thirteen years and multiple owners. As a first step and a way to build trust, Pete and C.H.I.'s management team embedded themselves in the daily hands-on operations of the company. Pete spent one week riding the delivery routes with C.H.I. truck drivers. Another week, he shadowed salespeople on the road. The idea was to identify pain points, such as inefficient delivery routes and scrap metal wastage, but also to become acquainted with the worker experience, listen to worker concerns and ideas (pillars one and two of the Win-Win workplace) and persuade workers to actively contribute to workplace change. Since profits from ownership stakes were not guaranteed, management also immediately took measures to demonstrate that the company was going to invest in the employees and include them in decision-making.

Pete and KKR approved a $1-million allocation to finance employee-recommended capital improvements at C.H.I. This was a clear sign of management's commitment to honoring employee voices. Employees first requested an air-conditioned factory, an unconventional investment for an open-floor, uninsulated plant. Nevertheless, KKR followed through on their commitment, and, sure enough, it proved advantageous as it maintained employee productivity during hot summers. In subsequent years, C.H.I. employees voted to invest in new break rooms, a new cafeteria with healthy food options, and an on-site medical clinic. Management additionally held financial literacy workshops where finance coaches helped workers understand their owner-ship stake—and also addressed their household finance questions. (Let's recall here that part of pillar one is to consider workers' lived reality outside the workplace.) A Zero-Sum leader might question whether these "extras" were smart investments; a Win-Win leader like Pete knows that they are. "How do you get workers to feel like they own their outcome and, together, we own this company and where it's headed? It's not just a handout of stock," Pete told me in our interview. "It's all of these things together that create an ownership culture among all of your workers."

The KKR and C.H.I. management team also established communication channels to build employee buy-in. They sought out employee-driven solutions such as reducing metal scrap waste and identifying delivery scheduling inefficiencies, resulting in reduced labor and fuel costs. Management began holding quarterly "owners' meetings" to keep the employee-feedback loop churning— "more feedback, more action, more feedback, more action" is how Pete described it—and to update all employees on the progress of the business. For example, safety improvements—including added machine guards and the mandatory use of goggles and steel-toed shoes freshly provided by the company—saw reportable injuries at the plant plummet by more than 50 percent, as did the severity of the injuries during the time that KKR owned C.H.I. "Over time, people felt invested in," Pete said. "And they felt like they could trust the leadership team."

Over its years of KKR ownership, C.H.I. paid four dividends to employees, amounting to around $9,000 apiece. Pete called the dividends a "moment of 'wow'" for workers who might have doubted their stock ownership would amount to anything. He remembers vividly the cumbersome—but oh-so-rewarding— process of paying out the stock when C.H.I. was sold in 2022. For C.H.I.'s eight hundred nonmanagement employees, the average payout on their ownership stake was $175,000, well in excess of the promised $15,000 minimum. Pete called some workers to confirm account numbers and to personally share the good news of the payout amount: "The assistant treasurer was just overcome with emotion of what this money was going to mean for his life. Many of these folks had not had wealth before. I heard stories of people who were going to get out of debt, pay off their home, be able to invest for the first time." On the other side of the ledger, the company reaped quantifiable benefit from prioritizing employee voices and well-being. C.H.I. cultivated a more engaged, satisfied, and productive workforce that reduced operational costs, preserved institutional knowledge (by improving retention), and drove the company's bottom-line success. The numbers punctuate Pete's story: C.H.I. saw profit margins swell from 20 percent to an impressive 35 percent—*and* realized a 120 percent surge in revenue—over the seven-year course of its transformation to a Win-Win workplace.

Process of Change: *Six Steps to Center Employee Voices*

Prepare

1. **Identify opportunities to center employee voice:** Recognize that traditional methods of gathering feedback haven't been effective. Employees currently feel like their voices don't matter. Look at your past employee engagement surveys to understand if participation rates and responses indicate that your workforce feels the same as the 76 percent of workers who told Gallup that their bosses don't care about worker well-being.

Act

2. **Prioritize centering employee voice:** Identify opportunities to integrate employee input and feedback across all aspects of the business value chain. Consider workers' lived experiences and expertise when making decisions. Create vehicles where employees can voice perceptions of their relationship with work. This should include soliciting their thoughts on the opportunities for the company to leverage relationships and their ideas for improvement. Model KKR's regularly held "owners' meetings" with a weekly standup or quarterly town hall to share examples of company performance, strategic initiatives, progress on employee initiatives, success stories, or cultural aspects. At the end of the day, branding

matters—and, ultimately, we want employees to think like owners and invest in company success as such.

Refine

3. **Engage with employees to develop new approaches to Win-Win working relationships:** Go beyond feedback boxes by giving employees a say and decision rights in developing new approaches to initiatives and programs that impact their work. For instance, in the KKR case, management allocated $1 million in their operational budget to funding improvements suggested by and voted on by employees, including air conditioning, delivery-route optimization, and an on-site medical clinic.

4. **Evaluate outcomes and adoption of new approaches:** Plumb employee opinion on the effectiveness of the changes and use regular meetings with your workforce to communicate the company perspective and discuss possible next steps. As KKR's Pete Stavros summarized this loop: "More feedback, more action, more feedback, more action."

5. **Adjust new approaches as needed:** Maintain open communication channels to gather ongoing employee feedback and collaboratively refine the implemented approaches to maximize effectiveness.

Communicate and Learn

6. **Communicate progress in implementing the new approaches, the results of the changes, and learnings from the actions:** Management at KKR and C.H.I. used their quarterly "owners' meetings" to update their entire workforce on how the company was doing, the progress of employee-suggested improvements, and the measured business impact of these improvements, including, for

example, increased productivity in summer months due to the new air-conditioning and cost-savings attributed to new delivery-route optimization.

The KKR case study provides real-world examples of strategies that embrace the cyclical Win-Win process of change and lead to a Win-Win workplace:

- **Committing to Win-Win working relationships and understanding employee concerns:** Pete Stavros's childhood experiences shaped his desire to improve the employer-employee dynamic. He recognized the negative impact of workers feeling undervalued. What are ways to get more proximate with your employees? Do your managers have the lived experience to relate not only to your customers but also to your employees—their staff?

- **Distributing leadership via entrepreneurial structures:** KKR transformed C.H.I. employees into owners, aligning employee and company goals. This fostered a sense of shared responsibility. We will explore more structures like this in Chapter Nine.

- **Reimagining employee benefits and investing in employee ideas:** KKR allocated $1 million for employee-selected improvements, demonstrating commitment to their voices.

- **Open communication channels:** KKR established systems for employees to propose ideas for mitigating financial and environmental costs, like reducing scrap metal waste and improving delivery routes.

- **Embracing transparency about human capital and measuring success:** KKR's aim was to have every worker's buy-in on the company's five-to-seven-year goals. That meant, in part, clearly communicating how individual roles contributed to the goal and identifying any skill gaps that needed to be addressed through training or development programs. This ensured each employee understood their unique role in achieving the company's vision. The company's profit margins and revenue increased significantly, highlighting the positive impact of centering employee voices.

Overall, these steps promote a culture of radical openness where employee feedback is actively sought, valued, and acted upon. It's not just a feel-good practice; it's a strategic imperative. In the most effective organizations these steps form a continuous cycle of improvement that allows the organization to unlock a wealth of untapped potential and build a more equitable future of work, where employee well-being and company success go hand in hand.

Now that we've learned about the importance of centering employee well-being, let's shift our focus to Chapter Two and committing to Win-Win working relationships.

CHAPTER TWO

COMMITTING TO WIN-WIN RELATIONSHIPS

White House correspondent Sandra Sobieraj Westfall was a typical Gen X working mom, juggling job and family and never letting the boss see her sweat. Then, in December 2013, she found herself without childcare on the morning of a big interview with Associate Justice Sonia Sotomayor at the Supreme Court. "I scrambled for a babysitter, even considered having the hotel concierge send a perfect stranger to my room to sit with my eight-year-old son Jonathan—anything but let my editor know that I had a personal conflict," Sandra, a veteran of the Associated Press and *People* magazine, recalled to me in a 2024 interview.[1] It was easier, she bargained, to let the justice know—and hope for the best.

In an email to Sotomayor's chambers staff, Sandra asked if Jonathan could tag along to the Supreme Court. "I apologized for being unprofessional, promised that Jonathan would sit quietly with his *Magic Tree House* books and not intrude on the justice's valuable time." The almost-instant reply left the desperate mom in tears. No, a staffer wrote back, Jonathan will not sit quietly in the lobby but instead will be the justice's special guest in her chambers where there were holiday decorations and hot chocolate. "I'll never forget this one line in the email: 'The justice doesn't believe anyone should have to apologize for being a parent.' That changed my life," Sandra told me. "It changed how I thought about being a mom who works and how I supervise other working parents."

NO MORE PRETENDING

Gone are the days of Sandra's Zero-Sum workplace, when baby boomer and Gen X employees were content to get a paycheck in exchange for getting a job done, usually within a set number of hours. Coming up in her career in the 1990s, when Washington journalism was still a male-dominated field, Sandra was also conditioned to expect that she needed to get her job done without her personal life getting in the way. But the Millennial and Gen Z majority of tomorrow's workforce doesn't live that way. They prioritize purpose, well-being, and alignment with personal values at work. This requires a fundamental change in how companies and organizations approach their employees.

Fostering Win-Win working relationships—ones that prioritize both company success and employee well-being by recognizing them as fully three-dimensional human beings—is the new way forward. The challenge, however, is that we have never been taught how to engage in relationships authentically at work. Instead, we are taught to act "professionally" and, in doing so, many workers silence big pieces of who they are or have felt silenced. A worker could be losing their home, caring for a chronically ill spouse, or taking three buses to work because their car broke down, and yet they put their game face on, come into work, and do their job—the stress and distraction of everything else be damned. Putting this artificial wall between work and life serves neither workers, nor their bosses, nor the company. In this chapter, we'll build on the information we learned in Chapter One to explore how we can fundamentally change workplace culture to embrace humanity and connection—across hierarchies, titles, departments, and identity markers.

Our artificial work personas have left our relationships at work—if we can call them that—frayed at best. One of my favorite Instagram accounts is called "Corporate Snark." Its description reads, "Work humor. I'm only saying what you already think." The account has almost three hundred thousand followers and posts daily videos of workplace scenarios that we all know too well: there's an employee jumping for joy when his weekly meeting with his boss is canceled, and a dog growling as he's persistently copied into irrelevant emails. While funny at first glance, the workplace videos and memes all over social media reflect the darker truth that many of our colleagues don't feel very collegial at work.[2]

It's hardly just an American problem. In fact, 84 percent of people in the United States and 93 percent of people in the United Kingdom reported working in a toxic work environment, according to surveys by FlexJobs and Gleeson Recruitment Group, a UK-based recruiting firm.[3] In China, after some CEOs publicly lauded the illegal "996 work culture," where people work a punishing 9 a.m. to 9 p.m., six days a week, the Chinese government took steps to tighten labor protections.[4] "Unlike their parents who believed that hard work pays off, there has been a growing sense of dissatisfaction among exhausted Chinese youth who see little reward in doing the same," the BBC reported from China in September 2021.[5] So-called right to disconnect legislation has similarly swept through Europe and is under consideration in Kenya. With France leading the way, a half-dozen European countries have, in recent years, enacted laws granting—and protecting—the rights of workers not to respond to work calls or emails during nonworking hours. Proponents cite the need to safeguard workers' mental health and family time and to avoid burnout. In the past, bosses most often brushed past these so-called lifestyle concerns, or outright ignored them, while workers learned "to go along to get along." They "transacted" with their colleagues, their supervisors, and senior management. They tolerated—and thus perpetuated—the Zero-Sum workplace.

HOW WE GOT HERE SHOWS THE WAY OUT

A brief look at history helps us understand how we got stuck in the Zero-Sum trap—and points the way to a Win-Win future. Our modern workplace was built from the vestiges of inherently inequitable systems. Workplace hierarchies, present-day management practices, and workplace organization were all established when businesses in the United States relied on the free labor of enslaved people.[6] This system was not created to treat people humanely, let alone consider them trustworthy or deserving of agency and choice. Instead, it was designed to eke out the most productivity possible from each human capital input. More plainly put, the system brutally (and literally) dehumanized workers by making them "property"—all in the name of profit. Vestiges of this still manifest themselves today in everything from the expectation of unpaid overtime to command-and-control structures and, inevitably, the "us against them" cultures and hierarchies that don't serve anyone. In short, for centuries, we have been raised in our professional lives to see work as impersonal and to objectify each other.

And none of this has been as good for business as we've been led to believe. Caitlin Rosenthal, a prominent professor of economic history, has made significant contributions to debunking the foundations of capitalist development and the theory that individual wealth accumulation will feed broader societal progress. Rosenthal observes, "Modern narratives of capitalist development often emphasize the positive-sum outcomes of many individual choices. They suggest that free, even selfish, decisions go hand in hand with growth and innovation. They also assume that vast wealth accumulated by a few accompanies improved circumstances for many."[7] None of this has been borne out. Drawing from the business history of the United States, Rosenthal makes clear the potential dangers of profit-seeking when everything, including human lives, is treated as a commodity.

Such is the inequity at the root of the disconnection and disaffection in the modern workplace. And, to continue the metaphor, it has sprouted realities like the 200 percent turnover rate in retail that is accepted as a given and built into retail operating and business models. Putting aside the moral implications of regarding workers as replaceable cogs in the machinery of business, consider the wasted cost of all that employee turnover. And what if that massive turnover wasn't a given, but an anomaly?

That's the future we are aiming for. Sebastian Buck, a cofounder of Enso Future Design who specializes in consulting with mission-driven organizations, has found—as I have in my own research—that efficiency and employee well-being do not have to be a trade-off. "In a drive for efficiency, which so often means limiting the very things that make work more fulfilling, enriching and joyful, leaders may curtail the very thing they are really looking for: financial health," Buck wrote in 2023. "But the most important hurdle to overcome in the quest for greater well-being is leaders' legacy attachment to prioritizing profit over people, leading to worse outcomes for both. Without real intention towards well-being, no progress is possible."[8] What does that intention look like, and is it worth it? Read on.

MY BOSS DOESN'T CARE ABOUT ME: THE DEMISE OF THE TRANSACTIONAL MODEL

Transactional relationships have brought the workforce to a pivotal juncture, culminating in the Great Resignation and its aftermath. The Great Resignation refers to a significant trend where large numbers of employees voluntarily left their jobs, often in response to shifts in the workplace brought about by the COVID-19 pandemic. These shifts included remote work opportunities, reevaluations of work-life balance, concerns over health and safety, and a reassessment of career priorities and values. Personal grievances that were once muted can now be endlessly aired and replayed on social media. The result is an environment that pits workers against workers, and also workers against their employers and companies. As you might recall from the Gallup poll discussed in Chapter One, a staggering 76 percent of workers feel profoundly neglected by their employers and believe their bosses do not genuinely care about them.[9] Contemplate the impact of spending a full third of one's life feeling unappreciated!

All of this raises a critical question for company leaders: When a workforce feels like its leaders don't care about them, why would workers care about the company's goals, strategic plans, and growth strategies? The traditional driver of loyalty—the paycheck—has lost its resonance. Wages are not keeping pace with inflation, and individuals are grappling with thirty-year-high household and student debt.[10] In this context, people are collectively reassessing the value of work. My research demonstrates that businesses benefit when employee-to-employee and employee-to-employer connections are optimized and everyone in the workplace feels like they can show up to work as their full selves and be regarded as full human beings.

PEOPLE DON'T QUIT JOBS; THEY QUIT *PEOPLE*

Typically, workers quit their jobs when they give up on the people in the workplace—peers and/or supervisors—because of the absence of any feeling of human connection to them. This underscores the imperative for companies—those who wish to retain their talent—to reflect seriously on the relational foundations that

WHAT THE RESEARCH SAYS

My analysis found that companies that cultivate a human-centered culture of connection financially outperform their industry peers. Data from 355 Fortune 500 firms revealed a strong correlation between positive employee relations—such as high employee engagement, low turnover rates, and comprehensive benefits packages—and robust financial metrics, including 46 percent of companies showed higher profitability, and 55 percent of companies have a strong performance in valuation and 55 percent of companies a strong performance in profits as a percentage of sales.

These companies experience a significant increase in valuation, indicating a rise in investor confidence and overall company worth—a strong foundation for future financial success. The companies also achieve a notable rise in revenue, suggesting increased productivity and a strong customer base. Furthermore, their assets show appreciable growth, further solidifying their financial strength. Many of these companies boast positive financial performance ratios relative to their peers, a strong indicator of overall profitability and efficiency.

Investing in employee well-being—through practices such as student loan debt forgiveness, as Abbott Laboratories offers, or the mental health wellness program that the Kimpton Hotel & Restaurant Group makes available to every single employee—is key to a Win-Win workplace culture of connection.[II] These practices can translate into a significant increase in their Living Wage Percentage (LWP), demonstrating a positive impact on their bottom line. LWP is a metric developed by JUST Capital, a nonprofit research organization that measures how well large US companies treat their workers across various factors, including wages. The LWP specifically focuses on the percentage of a company's full-time employees who are paid a localized living wage that allows a full-time worker to afford basic necessities like housing, food, childcare, and transportation in the community where they live. Additionally, these companies experience decreasing attrition rates, which translates to lower costs associated with employee turnover. This, along with the bold indicator of improved financial outcomes represented by reduced attrition wages, reflects the cost savings associated with retaining a happy and productive workforce.

By creating a Win-Win workplace that prioritizes both employee well-being and financial performance, companies can earn a loyal and productive workforce. This ultimately drives increased profitability and market value, benefiting both employees *and* the organization as a whole.

underpin their workplaces. The limitations of the transactional work culture are becoming increasingly apparent. When an organization is focused solely on cycles of short-term gains and output, then employee engagement, morale, and loyalty fall. What exactly do we mean by "employee engagement"? In a traditional Zero-Sum workplace, it is one-directional: the positive commitment demonstrated by employees toward their job and organization, and is an important asset for small and medium-sized enterprises that seek to adapt to an uncertain environment. But engagement in a Win-Win workplace is *bi*directional—or two-way and peer-oriented—where employees engage by having a say and decision rights on the issues that matter most to them and that impact their work performance and positive business results (e.g., increased profitability, productivity, customer loyalty).

A 2024 study by Gallup found that a mere 24 percent of American employees feel that their employers have their best interests at heart.[12] This translates into high turnover rates, a revolving door that costs companies between 50 and 200 percent of each lost employee's annual salary. Thus, a 100-person manufacturing organization offering an average salary of $50,000 and experiencing an average turnover between 28.6 percent and 40 percent could see turnover and replacement costs of approximately $660,000 to $2.86 million per year.[13]

Uncaring work environments hurt workers personally as well. People who experience incivility at work, such as sarcasm, demeaning interactions, interrupting, or rudeness, often suffer from stress and insomnia, according to research published in 2019 in *Occupational Health Science*.[14] Bad behavior by others on the job can also cause anxiety, fatigue, and even physical challenges like physical sickness and mental unwellness, as well as declines in productivity and morale, according to a 2018 Society for Human Resources Management Survey.[15] In that study, 66 percent of US workers attributed reduced productivity to incivility, while 59 percent believed incivility in the workplace saps employee morale. Figuring out how to work well with coworkers isn't just good for workers. It's critical for the financial health and well-being of the company.

Today's workforce craves work-life balance, mental health support, and the opportunity to contribute to something meaningful. Employees value autonomy and growth opportunities, and they are drawn to companies whose values resonate with their own. Furthermore, the rapid pace of technological change demands a shift from siloed work to collaborative innovation. Win-Win connections, built on trust and mutual respect and aligned with the Win-Win workplace pillars, foster the kind of teamwork necessary to cultivate this dynamic environment.

Case Study: *Ben & Jerry's Linked Prosperity*

In the dynamic landscape of corporate social responsibility, Ben & Jerry's has long been a beacon of innovation in social justice and the well-being of its employees and surrounding communities.

Founded on principles of equality and justice, the ice cream company has integrated these values into its business model, crafting a workplace culture that resonates deeply with its workforce. In this case study, we will show that social justice is an outcome of centering worker voices, as recommended in Chapter One, and of committing to a workplace culture of human connection, the topic of this chapter. Making a statement on a social justice issue is one thing—real transformation happens when we ensure that employees can bring their full selves to work 52 weeks a year as part of a sustainable operational business model.

Ben & Jerry's outward-facing work in social justice is well known. Lesser known is the company's internal commitment to equity as it aims to create prosperity for everyone connected to the business. For Ben & Jerry's, the most important ingredient is people. As cofounder Jerry Greenfield shared with me: "We've always believed that our success is directly linked to the well-being of our employees. When our employees feel valued, respected and heard, they're more engaged, more creative, and, ultimately, help us deliver the best possible products and experiences to our customers. We call it 'linked prosperity'—the idea that our business can't be successful unless our employees, our suppliers, our neighbors, and our environment are all thriving too, creating a win-win situation for everyone connected to the business."[16] This understanding forms the backbone and engine of the company's business model, leading to a strong financial performance, a loyal customer base, and an overall competitive advantage.

Ben & Jerry's concept of linked prosperity means that the success of the business should be shared with everyone involved in making its ice cream. It's a move away from the traditional business model that solely focuses on maximizing profit for shareholders.

Ben & Jerry's goes beyond just offering competitive wages. They provide a comprehensive benefits package (health insurance, paid time off, gym memberships) and even fun perks like free ice cream. This shows the company values its employees' well-being and financial security while also recognizing their contribution to the company's success. Additionally, Ben & Jerry's has offered Employee Stock Ownership Plans (ESOPs) in the past, directly linking worker fortunes to the company's performance. This combination of competitive pay, benefits, perks, and a potential ownership stake exemplifies its commitment to linked prosperity for the internal team.

Here are some examples of how Ben & Jerry's puts this into action in its larger community:

- **Fairtrade ingredients:** Ben & Jerry's sources many key ingredients like cocoa, coffee, and sugar through Fairtrade certification. This ensures farmers get a fair price for their crops, along with an additional premium that can be used to improve their communities.[17]
- **Supporting dairy workers:** Ben & Jerry's pays dairy farmers a premium above the market rate for their milk. This extra money can be used for better wages, improved working conditions, or investments in the farm itself.[18]
- **Community focus:** Ben & Jerry's supports social justice causes through their foundation, using their resources to raise awareness and advocate for positive change.

Overall, linked prosperity aims to create a more sustainable and equitable business model. By ensuring everyone involved is treated fairly, Ben & Jerry's believes they can create a better product and a stronger company in the long run.

Ben & Jerry's aims to have a workforce that shares in its mission and its success—and reflects the diversity of its customers—helps the company foster a sustainable business model in the following ways:

- **Innovation:** A diverse workforce that is encouraged (a) to bring their whole selves to the job and (b) to leverage their lived experiences, offering the company a wider range of ideas for its success.
- **Employee retention:** Feeling valued and seen as a peer contributor to core business leads to higher employee satisfaction and retention, reducing recruitment and training costs.
- **Market relevance:** Understanding the needs of diverse communities through a culture of communication and connection with their employees allows the company, with employee input, to develop products and messaging that resonate with a broader audience.

Moreover, Ben & Jerry's has, since 1988, taken a transparent approach to tracking and reporting their financials and their programs—another key to a Win-Win workplace and one we'll discuss more in Chapter Eight. The company's Social & Environmental Assessment Report (SEAR) includes a third-party review of the company's priorities for each year, and all of this information is publicly available on the company website. The impact is evident, with $8.6 billion in revenue in 2023 and an operating margin of 10.8 percent. Ben & Jerry's continues to achieve its goal and mission of sustainable growth. We will discuss in Chapter Ten how to follow this example to measure impact and return on investment in the Win-Win workplace.

The key to lasting change lies in weaving these actions into programs and policies, the very fabric of the organization. How a company evaluates employees, conducts interviews, and even celebrates success can all be transformed to reflect a focus on well-being and growth. We need to move beyond symbolic gestures and ensure that everyday practices embody the company's stated values. The modern workforce has options that they are exercising in unprecedented ways. Top performers seek out environments that prioritize their well-being and growth. A culture of fear is a recipe for mediocrity, not excellence.

Company culture can make the difference between losing and attracting new employees who believe in the mission more than a paycheck. When a company successfully brands its culture by promoting its values, it reaps vast rewards. Employees aligned with the vision flock to the company, work with enthusiasm, and communicate the company's virtues. Culture *is* strategy.

Jobina's Story: *Empty Words versus Action*

For many years, Jobina Gonsalves enjoyed a thriving career as head of human resources for Bosch in Singapore. Despite being an outsider (Jobina is Indian), she told me in a 2023 interview that she initially felt well supported by her team and business.[19] Bosch had openly pledged its commitment to diversity and cross-cultural communication. In addition, Bosch was global and boasted that "encouraging a free exchange of ideas between people of different cultures would only expand its reach and marketability." It was everything Jobina wanted to hear.

But over time, Jobina experienced that innovation was rare and negative stereotyping was rampant. At one point, Jobina was told by a supervisor that she would not "get the acceptance" she needed to become "an Indian leader in a Chinese society in Singapore." The reality was the company culture did not match its stated values, and Jobina knew it. "The culture that I saw my manager propagating was not aligned with my values," she told me. "The color of my passport should not define how good or bad I am."

Still, Jobina was not looking for a new job when a headhunter approached her about a position opening at TÜV SÜD, a company that offers safety testing, inspection, and certification globally. The headhunter sold her on the potential of the position: TÜV SÜD touched on all industries, all verticals. TÜV SÜD was deeply long-term oriented and focused on investing in its current workforce and attracting those with similar values as their culture of innovation and employee empowerment. TÜV SÜD cared about all aspects of workplace safety including physiological safety and diversity. However, Jobina was skeptical. She'd heard these same claims from Bosch.

But during her first job interview there, Jobina realized TÜV SÜD was different. Everyone she spoke with seemed to identify with the *purpose* of the organization more so than their paychecks. Whereas the average tenure of a C-suite executive is 4.9 years globally, TÜV SÜD's executives average a tenure of more than a decade. When Jobina accepted the position, she spent her first day in the company's German headquarters; on her floor she found colleagues of twenty-two different nationalities. But her real confirmation that TÜV SÜD lived by its values was when Jobina announced she wanted to move from leading the Asia Pacific Human Resources Division to something different at the global level. Nobody tried to pigeonhole her or dissuade her from trying. Instead, others encouraged her to follow her passion. "So long as I was able to get out of my comfort zone and raise my hand for stretch projects, I had the chance. I think that's the reason why I'm still here," Jobina told me, "because I got that chance to try something different and be adventurous, and the company was always supportive."

Jobina's experience is revealing. At her previous company, the disconnect between the company's stated values of "innovation" and "employee empowerment" and its actual culture felt stark. From her perspective, that culture resulted in centralized decision-making. Jobina felt disengaged and unfulfilled, ultimately leading her to seek employment elsewhere.

THE POWER OF RELATIONAL COMPANY CULTURE

A strong relational company culture is a strategic advantage in the modern workplace. As Peter Drucker famously said, "Culture eats strategy for breakfast." Based on my research and work, a relational company culture is one built on the following foundations:

- **Trust:** Fostering open communication and psychological safety.
- **Shared values:** Ensuring company values are not just words on a poster but core principles reflected in actions.
- **Open communication:** Creating an environment where employees feel comfortable sharing ideas and concerns.

Jobina's experience at TÜV SÜD exemplifies the power of a relational company culture. The company's focus on employee well-being, long-term development, and global perspectives resonated deeply with her. Open communication channels allowed her to share her ideas and concerns, and she felt valued and supported. This sense of belonging and purpose significantly enhanced her work experience.

THE BENEFITS OF A WIN-WIN CULTURE OF CONNECTION

The benefits of Win-Win relationships extend far beyond employee satisfaction and include the following:

- **Increased employee engagement:** Employees who feel valued and supported are more likely to be engaged in their work.
- **Enhanced productivity:** A happy and motivated workforce is a productive workforce.

- **Reduced turnover:** Win-Win relationships lead to a more loyal workforce, reducing the costs associated with recruiting and training new employees.

Compared with workers at low-trust, Zero-Sum workplaces, employees at high-trust companies report 74 percent less stress; 106 percent more energy at work; 50 percent higher productivity; 13 percent fewer sick days; 76 percent more positive interaction with their job and organization; 29 percent more satisfaction with their lives overall, and 40 percent less burnout.[20] This translates into significant cost savings for companies, since retaining talent is far more cost-effective than recruiting and training new employees.

To move past this mindset, we need to restore humanity to the workplace. This means prioritizing employee voices and well-being, as we discussed in Chapter One. It also means learning a new way to work. But what does it mean to be human at work—and to build Win-Win relationships? What types of practices and organizational design strategies lead to the creation of unique and successful work cultures? Both Jobina's experience and the Ben & Jerry's case study provide real-world examples of strategies for getting to a Win-Win workplace boosted by the connective tissue of a high-functioning team pulling in the same direction—toward collective success! Here's how you can get there too.

Process of Change: *Six Steps to Build a Culture of Human-Centered Connection*

Prepare

1. **Start by centering employee voices:** Create vehicles for surfacing, illuminating, and understanding what employees think of the existing workplace culture. What are their

perceptions of what's "professional" and what unwritten rules exist about how they are expected to show up at work? Which boundaries, rules, and expectations work for your employees, and which cause problems? Before you can solve problems and build a more productive and human-centered culture, you need to understand the full perspective of your workforce and what policies and behaviors need to change.

Act

2. **Commit to a Win-Win culture of connection:** Be guided by employee feedback to cultivate a clear vision for Win-Win relationships and ensure your company values promote collaboration and care. Involve employees in shaping this vision—their voices matter!

Refine

3. **Engage with employees to develop new approaches to Win-Win working relationships:** Go beyond feedback boxes by giving employees a say and decision rights in developing new initiatives and programs that matter most to them and impact their work as new circumstances and concerns arise. For example, it was not part of the Ben & Jerry's employee well-being strategy to bring in unions. But when 40 workers in a Ben & Jerry's store in Vermont voted in 2023 to unionize, the company leadership had a choice to make: Are they really "linked" to their workforce or is that just talk? Leadership responded to the unionization overture by stepping up and supporting the workers' desire to unionize.[21] A spokesperson for Ben & Jerry's said, "To recognize and support the rights of the workers at the Burlington store to unionize and collectively bargain is consistent with Ben & Jerry's progressive values and three-part mission. We're appreciative that this has been a collaborative and respectful process through which

the scoopers were fully engaged."[22] This shows the durability of the Win-Win workplace pillars in Ben & Jerry's business model. Since its founding as a private company in 1978, to going public in 1985, then becoming a wholly owned subsidiary of Unilever in 2000 and, finally, to the latest unionizing in 2024, the Win-Win culture of human-centered connection and working relationships has persisted.[23]

4. **Evaluate outcomes and adoption of the new approaches:** Collect feedback through regular surveys and focus groups, monitor participation and engagement in activities, and assess impact using key performance indicators such as employee satisfaction and team cohesion. For example, Ben & Jerry's evaluates the effectiveness of its "linked prosperity" approach by gathering feedback on their benefits package and monitoring participation in ESOPs, ensuring employees feel valued and invested in the company's success.

5. **Adjust the new approaches as needed:** Hold feedback sessions to discuss improvements, analyze data to identify areas for adjustment, and implement iterative changes. Engage employee champions to support the changes and communicate transparently about any adjustments. For instance, Ben & Jerry's continuously engages with employees to refine their benefits and perks, such as free ice cream and health benefits, ensuring they remain relevant and valuable. This ongoing feedback helps the company improve and expand the impact of its linked prosperity model.

Communicate and Learn

6. **Communicate progress in implementing the new approaches, the results of the changes, and learnings from the actions:** Engage with employees along with external stakeholders in this communication.

OVERCOMING CHALLENGES AND BUILDING FOR THE FUTURE

Implementing the Win-Win workplace pillars doesn't come without challenges. Budget constraints, cultural resistance, and metrics for success can all be hurdles. However, companies can build a strong business case for change by demonstrating the return on investment in terms of employee retention and productivity. Open communication that invites employees to contribute to the workplace process and policy development can help increase strategic and cultural alignment while ensuring that everyone embraces Win-Win practices.

Win-Win relationships and a culture of human-centered connection are a sure formula for increased productivity and employee retention. Beyond that, a deeper benefit may be in fostering human potential. By prioritizing well-being and purpose, companies can tap into a wellspring of creativity, innovation, and resilience. Employees who feel valued and empowered will not just be productive; they will also be passionate contributors, driven by a desire to make a difference in the organization's competitiveness, market share, profitability, responsibility, sales, and overall success. In my research to develop the Win-Win workplace pillars, I saw quantifiable evidence that less hierarchical organizations see benefits to the bottom line. In the analysis of data from the American Opportunity Index and firm financial performance described in the previous chapter, I found evidence that firms with higher median wages—controlling for differences across industries and occupations—and higher percentages of US workers earning a living wage see tangible, positive returns to their investments in terms of revenue and profit and have better culture and employee relationships.

In this chapter, we learned how Win-Win workplaces transform hierarchical, supervision-oriented relationships into ones based on transparency, deep respect, and alignment, which are drivers of success. Here, both employees and the business thrive.

In Chapter Three, we'll delve into the concept of intersectional inclusion. This exploration aims to shed light on how an employee's life outside of work impacts their performance. We'll offer strategies to overcome potential barriers and foster a fair and dynamic environment that promotes individual growth and overall business success. . . . Let's jump in!

CHAPTER THREE

THE WHOLE EMPLOYEE

HOW INTERSECTIONAL INCLUSION UNLOCKS POTENTIAL

Imagine a team developing a fitness app.

A leader in a Zero-Sum workplace would think only about team members' skills, looking for a developer, a marketer, and a designer. That leader would set a deadline and wait for the results.

Win-Win leaders, on the other hand, would look much deeper. They would still need a developer, of course, but they'd also think about what else that developer brings to the table. A developer with a physical disability, for example, might help to ensure that the team doesn't inadvertently create a product that is ableist. A marketer who is a mother could ensure that the product speaks in a relatable way to its prospective audience. In other words, Win-Win leaders look at the whole person and the three-dimensional contributions that person can make to the team, based on their backgrounds and lived realities. To Win-Win leaders, employees are not just bodies to fill slots on a roster.

For too long, firms have been afraid to consider demographics in forming a team. Yet research consistently shows that diverse teams outperform nondiverse ones: they generate more and better ideas and offer insights on accessibility, functionality, and new target consumer audiences that less diverse teams might miss.[1]

Team members' combined identities create a valuable perspective that strengthens the final product and the sales strategy. By understanding and leveraging these intersections in identities, companies can foster innovation and success.

WHAT IS INTERSECTIONALITY, AND HOW CAN IT WORK FOR YOU?

"Intersectionality," a term coined by legal scholar Kimberlé Crenshaw in 1989, originally emerged from feminist theory and activism to address the unique experiences of Black women who faced intersecting forms of discrimination based on race and gender.[2] At its core, intersectionality recognizes that individuals hold multiple social identities—such as race, gender, class, sexuality, disability, etc.—that intersect and interact with each other, shaping their experience in unique and profound ways.

The Win-Win process of change champions intersectional exploration and aims to illuminate how all employees' identities and lives outside of work influence their performance inside the workplace. When employees are on the job, they often play multiple roles and possess various identities. And yet these complexities are often overlooked, reducing individuals to only one identity, like their race or gender. Features central to a person's identity such as caregiving responsibilities, religious beliefs, or physical abilities may go unnoticed unless employers, managers, and colleagues actively create an environment where the whole person and the whole person's reality can be acknowledged. For instance, a veteran without a college degree but with valuable experience gained during service, possibly struggling with post-traumatic stress disorder, brings a unique perspective and may face unique challenges.

Creating an intersectional workplace—one that, keeping with our example, can tap the veteran's unique experience and perspective while also accommodating their unique challenges—requires more than just flexible policies. It's about fostering a sense of community and acceptance. By recognizing the richness of employee identities and the value they bring, companies can combat burnout and create a truly inclusive environment.

This requires investment in strategies that go beyond traditional top-down diversity equity, and inclusion (DEI) approaches. A nuanced understanding of employee needs, across all intersections, is key to building a workplace where every voice is valued and contributes to business success. Alternatively, when employers miss the opportunities presented by their employees' intersectional identities, they risk losing the upside potential of employee insights to the business—and also risk losing high-potential talent.

Case Study: *Hidden Costs of Hidden Identities*

At thirty-two, Gerald Singer was a veteran transitioning back to civilian life after serving in the US Army. While his military service had equipped him with valuable skills, finding fulfilling work proved difficult. After a string of minimum-wage jobs, he finally landed a role in a field that utilized his strengths: logistics. Tracking inventory for the manufacturing plant felt familiar, like managing supplies for his platoon. He excelled at scheduling and organizing shipments, maximizing efficiency, and leveraging his team's strengths, just like he did in the military.

Despite his dedication to the job and positive attitude, Gerald's punctuality mysteriously declined four months into his tenure. Genevieve Richards, his manager, shared that she believed in understanding her employees and addressing issues directly. However, the company's strict, no-fault attendance policy left little room for flexibility. After several late arrivals, Genevieve recalled to me in an interview that she "felt obligated" to initiate disciplinary action.[3]

One day, while on break, Genevieve said she noticed Gerald sprinting from the bus stop, sweaty and out of breath. This sparked a conversation that revealed the root of his tardiness: car trouble. As the sole provider for his family, Gerald didn't have room in his budget for car repairs. Instead, drawing on his military resourcefulness, he sketched out a schedule for taking the bus to work. What was normally a thirty-minute commute by car now required one bus transfer and took almost two hours door-to-door. Worse, his meticulously planned schedule depended on the bus running on time—a gamble he often lost.

When buses were delayed, he would end up running into the building worrying that he'd be late and lose his job. So, he ran like his life depended on it because his livelihood *did*.

With each explanation, Genevieve "felt a growing sense of regret," she recalled to me months later. Her focus on performance hadn't considered that Gerald faced challenges outside of work. Before his late streak, she hadn't even known he was a veteran. While she'd noticed his discipline and respect for authority, she hadn't delved deeper or offered support. Now, with disciplinary action underway, Genevieve said she realized that she and the company "had missed an opportunity to help a valuable employee" through a temporary hardship.

HIDDEN STRUGGLES IN THE WORKPLACE

The challenges employees face reach far beyond securing reliable transportation. Workers in the United States and across the globe are facing myriad issues that may not surface in workplace conversation but occupy a significant proportion of their active thoughts. Here are a few examples of what employees may be coping with on a daily basis:

- Approximately 600 million working-age adults worldwide— or 17 percent of the world's working-age population— provide care to children, older adults, and people with disabilities or chronic illnesses, reports the International Labor Organization.[4]

- In 2021, Feeding America projected that 42 million Americans (one in eight) would experience food insecurity that year, and the Urban Institute reported 17 percent of fully employed workers experienced food insecurity in 2022.[5]
- Half of adults living in homeless shelters and almost two-fifths of people sleeping on the streets had jobs during the year they experienced homelessness according to a 2021 report.[6]
- The World Health Organization estimates that one in four people in the world will be affected by mental or neurological disorders at some point in their lives.[7]
- Multiple studies have found that members of Gen Z tend to report more mental illness than prior generations, with one study finding 42 percent of Gen Z has a self-reported mental health condition.[8]

Right now, conversations about food insecurity, homelessness, mental illness, or caring for ailing family members are scarce in the workplace, and few workplaces normalize discussion of these issues. Destigmatizing these topics may help employees feel more understood at work. And managers can start to build a workplace culture of openness by leading by example and enabling corporations to evolve from Zero-Sum workplaces to Win-Win workplaces.

UNDERSTANDING THE STRANGER BESIDE YOU

How well do any of us *really* know our colleagues? Do you know if the person that greets you at the front desk had another career prior to their current role? Or if they are attending night school? Do you know if the person who fixes the printer when it gets jammed also jams in a jazz band during their spare time? Whether they are planning for their first child? These may seem frivolous questions, but they lead to an important, broader question: What is beneath the surface of your workforce, and what motivates and interests them?

A staggering 82 percent of employees indicate that it is important for their organization to see them as a person, not merely an employee.[9] And yet only 45 percent of employees believe their organizations actually see them as more than just a worker.[10] To foster an effective workplace, this gap must be closed.

For Gerald, getting to work every day was complicated by his socioeconomic status: His inability to afford car repairs impacted his attendance, the age of his vehicle made it more prone to breakdown, and an upgrade was cost-prohibitive with his income. Yet, he chose to sprint instead of sitting down with his manager Genevieve to discuss his troubles.

Consider his behavior in light of a study published in the *Journal of Business and Psychology* that found employees who reported higher levels of financial stress were more likely to conceal their struggles from colleagues and employers. These strategies mirror those used by members of other marginalized groups to evade stereotypes and stigma in the workplace. Employees would avoid discussing financial struggles, downplay their material possessions, or adopt frugal behaviors to avoid being perceived as financially irresponsible. In turn, the study found engaging in such financial hiding behaviors correlated with reports of lower job satisfaction and greater psychological distress. Another study, published in the *Journal of Applied Psychology*, found that employees who were struggling with debt were more likely to experience "debt-related stress," which was associated with lower job performance, lower job satisfaction, and higher turnover intentions.

Moreover, the onus of transportation costs is not borne equally across the workforce. Many leaders and people in management rarely think twice about how they get to work. Genevieve didn't. Sure, higher-level employees lament days of heavy traffic and increasing gas prices, but their transportation costs do not account for a significant percentage of their take-home pay. Globally, however, workers spend between 15 and 29 percent of their after-tax income on transportation, making it one of the top expenses behind housing.[11] In October 2023, the *New York Times* wrote on its front page about the growing trend of workers living in their cars because they cannot afford rent.[12]

Hierarchical structures complicate opportunities for many higher-level executives to gain the personal connection needed to empathize with or understand the diverse experiences and challenges that their employees face outside of work or how those experiences may affect their job performance. This is a problem because, on average, most people spend one-third of their lives at work. And so, any problems outside of work—like housing insecurity—become the company's problem. Personal challenges result in a phenomenon called "presenteeism," when employees show up to work sick, exhausted, or too distracted by personal issues to focus on their workload, which can ultimately be costlier than absenteeism.[13]

Don't underestimate the iceberg effect of presenteeism. It's like an athlete showing up to a race with a fever. You might be physically present, but your performance suffers. We see this in several ways:

- **Productivity plummets:** Presentee employees struggle to focus, make more mistakes, and often have to redo work.[14]
- **Costs balloon:** Fixing those errors takes time and resources. Plus, missed deadlines and needing extra help from colleagues are a hidden drain on the bottom line.[15]
- **The sickness spreads:** When people come in sick physically and mentally, it has a domino effect. Colleagues are

impacted, leading to more absences and productivity declines.[16]

The research is clear: presenteeism can be ten times more costly than absenteeism. Think about it: replacing an employee costs between 50 and 200 percent of an employee's annual salary, while presenteeism can quietly chip away at profits year after year.[17]

The good news? Supportive workplace policies that allow employees to show up fully are the ultimate Win-Win. When employees feel valued and empowered to take care of themselves, it boosts both their well-being and the company's performance.

THE POWER OF UNDERSTANDING THE WHOLE EMPLOYEE

Recognizing and embracing the lived realities of employees can be a powerful catalyst for organizational success. When leaders take the time to understand the personal challenges their team members face and encourage open communication, they can unlock new levels of engagement and innovation. Consider the story of Yamini Rangan, CEO of HubSpot, the leading software company that provides a comprehensive platform for inbound marketing, sales, and customer service. Her journey from rural India to the helm of a $30 billion company underscores the profound impact of authenticity and resilience. Her leadership demonstrates how recognizing and valuing the diverse backgrounds and strengths of employees can transform a company's culture and drive exceptional results.

Yamini's Story: *The Impact of Authenticity*

Yamini Rangan's path to the C-suite makes a case for intersectional strategies applying her lived experience growing up and training as an engineer to help her become a top salesperson. Growing up in a small town without a high school, her initial focus was simply on completing her education. "All I was thinking about is, like, how am I going to get to high school and finish high school, much less thinking about running a multi-billion-dollar company," she shared during a 2023 interview.[18] Yet, her relentless curiosity and love of learning propelled her forward. "My journey has been completely unplanned, completely accidental, in many cases, but I would say that maybe, I had one thing, curiosity and love of learning, and that has been my entire journey."[19]

Her career took a significant turn during the 2001 recession when she was forced to pivot from a marketing role to sales. "When I showed up the first day of my marketing career, they said, 'Well, we don't have the job anymore. You're in sales now.'" With no experience in sales, she drew on what she already knew. "I treated sales like an engineering problem . . . and that helped me become a better salesperson, not the regular way of how people were doing it. And honestly, I've learned that you just have to be authentic and lean into your own strengths."

The cultural landscape of the position was also new to Yamini. "The first thing that you do, you look at a room full of people that don't look like you. They're not Indian; they're not women. But they're all successful," she shared. "And you start to think about, how do I follow their journey?" Sports looked like an in-road with her new colleagues, she said, but she was no good at golf—or even watching *Sunday Night Football*. "I decided very early in my career in sales, in tech, that I was just going to stand out rather than fit in."[20]

When Yamini was unexpectedly tapped to lead HubSpot after former CEO Brian Halligan experienced an accident, she focused on a future-oriented vision: "The first thing that happens . . . is like the imposter syndrome, like, 'Am I going to be able to do it? Can I step in [after] someone who's been a visionary, who's done such a phenomenal job with the company?' You start to ask all of those questions. Now, I found in my career that those questions are just wasted energy. Doesn't help you, does not help the company, does not help with the cause that you're trying to do."[2] Instead, she asked herself, "What do I care about the most if I've been tapped into this opportunity?" Her answer: making HubSpot a better company, fostering a better culture, promoting diversity in tech, and being present with her family. "Every action I take is aligned with those four things that I want to accomplish. It's not based on the past. It's not based on who was in the role and how amazing he was in the role. It's about the future that I am committed to creating, and that changes the journey."

Yamini's approach to company culture is dynamic and adaptive, much like a product that evolves based on user feedback. "At HubSpot, we think about culture as yet another product. And what happens with your product? Your product doesn't remain the same for years in a row. You're constantly evolving the product, and for us, we are constantly evolving culture." She compared this part of her role to that of a product manager for culture, asking, "What is the best feature and what's the most requested feature?" This mindset has led to significant shifts, such as transitioning from a predominantly in-office workforce to one where 88 percent of employees now work from home or have flexible arrangements.

Leveraging employee identities as a competitive advantage is not a mere initiative at HubSpot; it's part of the company's DNA. "It's absolutely intentional. . . . We build products to serve communities, and if we cannot represent how the communities represent themselves, then bias actually enters," Yamini explained. This commitment is reflected in HubSpot's leadership, which is 50 percent women, and its board, which is 60 percent women and people of color. "I started in the tech industry in the mid-nineties, and it did not look like this," she shared.

Yamini's conviction about the benefit of having employees with a broad range of perspectives and experiences is unequivocal:

"I'm done trying to prove diversity with data, we just need to be diverse. That's it." For her, the imperative is clear: diversity is not just about numbers but about creating an environment where all employees can bring their whole selves and range of identities to work, fostering innovation, and better serving customers.

Yamini's leadership at HubSpot illustrates the profound impact of authenticity, operationalizing the value of interesting identities, and continuously ensuring that the company culture meets the needs of both employees and the customer they serve. Her journey and insights offer a powerful reminder that when leaders bring their whole selves and intersectional identities to work, they unlock not just individual potential but collective success.

WHOLE SELVES AND ECONOMIC RETURNS: WHAT THE DATA SHOW

Leveraging employees' intersecting identities and lived experiences can profoundly enhance innovation and inclusion within a company, yielding both creative and economic benefits. Research consistently shows that, compared to homogeneous teams, diverse teams excel in problem-solving and innovation by bringing a broader range of perspectives and approaches to the table. In 2019, McKinsey & Company found that in terms ethnic and cultural diversity, top-quartile companies outperformed those in the fourth one by 36 percent in profitability.[22] Additionally, research suggests that integrating neurodiversity into leadership teams can help organizations access untapped potential and other benefits. Research in the *Harvard Business Review* found that teams including neuro-minorities, such as employees with ADHD or dyslexia, had a stronger potential to yield unique ideas and groundbreaking solutions to problems.[23]

Consider this: Several highly successful CEOs, including Charles Schwab, Elon Musk, and Richard Branson, are reported to be neurodivergent.[24] Collectively, their companies boast a net worth exceeding $1 trillion. However, within the broader workforce, only 1 percent of corporate managers identify as neurodivergent, compared to an estimated 10 to 20 percent prevalence in the general population.[25] This stark discrepancy suggests either that neurodivergent individuals are actively concealing their neurodivergence or they are being overlooked for leadership positions. The missed potential extends beyond neurodiversity. Companies that fail to create inclusive environments where employees feel comfortable revealing their full identities—their neurodiversity, ethnicity, gender identity, and the intersections of these identities—are missing out on a significant pool of top talent.[26]

By harnessing the unique skills and backgrounds of employees from different walks of life, organizations can foster a culture of creativity and adaptability that also improves employee morale and retention rates. Studies have shown that inclusive workplaces see higher levels of employee engagement and satisfaction, leading to reduced turnover and increased productivity. Furthermore, companies that prioritize diversity and inclusion often experience better financial performance, as diverse teams are more adept at understanding and meeting the needs of a diverse customer base.[27]

Process of Change: *Six Steps to Build an Intersectional Workplace*

Prepare

1. **Identify opportunities to center employee voice:** Conduct surveys or hold focus groups that ask employees about their lived experiences at work. How do their identities (caregiver, neurodiversity, geographical upbringing, etc.) intersect and influence their work experience?

WHAT THE RESEARCH SAYS

From my analysis of data from 355 Fortune 500 firms, implementing intersectional inclusion strategies focusing on gender and racial equality can lead to a Win-Win workplace with numerous benefits:

1. **Diverse and inclusive workplace:** These strategies promote diversity, bringing a variety of perspectives and ideas. This diversity fosters innovation and creativity within the company.

2. **Long-term employee engagement:** Promoting gender equality in promotions and striving for parity among racial and ethnic groups can enhance long-term employee engagement. Employees who perceive fairness and equal opportunities are more likely to remain with the company, thereby reducing turnover rates and associated costs.

3. **Ethical and social responsibility:** Companies prioritizing intersectional inclusion demonstrate commitment to ethical practices and social responsibility. This enhances their reputation among stakeholders, including customers, investors, and the broader community.

4. **Legal compliance:** Addressing issues related to pay equity and diversity targets not only improves company culture but also ensures compliance with legal requirements. This proactive approach can mitigate legal risks and potential liabilities associated with discrimination lawsuits.

Additionally, 37 percent of companies implementing intersectional inclusion strategies have a strong performance in assets and 42 percent of companies with a strong performance in intersectional have a strong performance in valuation showing a correlation to business success.

Act

2. **Setting up intersectional inclusion strategies:** Traditional DEI often focuses on broad categories, which can miss the specific needs of individuals. Intersectional inclusion strategies aim to address this by recognizing that everyone has unique experiences shaped by various lived experiences.

   - **Design targeted initiatives:** Based on your audit and employee feedback, design specific programs and policies that address identified issues. This could involve unconscious bias training, mentoring programs for underrepresented groups, or flexible work arrangements that cater to diverse needs.
   - **Normalize open communication:** Create a safe space for employees to share personal challenges without fear of judgment. This could involve offering confidential support channels (like an Employee Assistance Program) or anonymous feedback mechanisms.
   - **Challenge assumptions:** Train managers and leaders to recognize that seemingly universal experiences can be very different for various employees. A quiet work environment might be ideal for someone with neurodivergence but isolating for someone else.

Refine

3. **Engage with employees to develop new approaches to intersectional inclusion strategies:**

   - **Focus on strengths-based inclusion:** Identify the unique strengths and perspectives that neurodivergent employees or those facing personal challenges can bring to the table. Yamini Rangan's story highlights the value of leveraging unique strengths. She didn't try to fit in by playing golf, but instead used her engineering background to excel in sales. This aligns with the concept of focusing on the strengths that employees bring based on their experiences and identities.

- **Employee resource groups (ERGs) as champions:** Empower existing ERGs or create new ones to play a key role in identifying intersectional needs and advocating for solutions. ERGs provide a space for employees to share experiences, identify challenges, and propose solutions.
- **Actively destigmatize vulnerability:** Promote open communication about personal challenges. Encourage employees to share their experiences through storytelling workshops or anonymous support groups, fostering a sense of community and reducing shame.

4. **Evaluate outcomes and adoption of new approaches:** Based on employee feedback and data analysis, be prepared to adapt and improve your intersectional strategies. This demonstrates a commitment to continuous learning and growth.

- **Metrics and data analysis:** Establish clear metrics to track progress on intersectional inclusion goals. This could involve employee surveys on well-being, retention rates for diverse groups, or promotion rates across demographics.
- **Focus group discussions:** After piloting new approaches, conduct follow-up discussions with focus groups to understand employee experiences and gather feedback on the effectiveness of the strategies.
- **Review feedback:** Regularly collect feedback from ERGs on the impact of intersectional initiatives on their specific needs and concerns.

5. **Adjust new approaches as needed:** Maintain open communication channels to gather ongoing employee feedback

and collaboratively refine the implemented approaches to maximize effectiveness.

Communicate and Learn

6. **Communicate progress in implementing the new approaches, the results, and learnings:**

- **Showcase success stories:** Highlight examples of how intersectional inclusion has benefited both employees and the company. This can inspire others and demonstrate the value of these strategies.
- **Celebrate employee vulnerability:** Recognize and appreciate employees who share their vulnerabilities and personal experiences. This demonstrates the company's commitment to creating a safe and inclusive space for everyone. Recall how Yamini articulated her four priorities in her role, which included being present as a parent. We need to allow others to personalize their goals and reasons for work.
- **Normalize "bringing your whole self" to work:** Through storytelling, internal communication campaigns, and leadership actions, create a culture where employees feel comfortable being their authentic selves at work. When Yamini, as HubSpot CEO, transitioned from a predominantly in-office workforce to a flexible work model, she leveraged the strengths of a diverse team and created a culture that fosters innovation and better serves customers. This approach aligns with the concept of "bringing your whole self" to work and demonstrates the positive outcomes of intersectional inclusion.

In this chapter, we learned how intersectionality helps companies move beyond mere compliance with diversity goals to harness the full potential of a truly inclusive workforce. It fosters innovation, strengthens market reach, and ultimately leads to a more successful and sustainable business. On the other side of the ledger, intersectional inclusion leads to higher employee satisfaction, engagement, productivity and—again—business success.

Now that we've covered how intersectionality, inclusion, and an understanding of employees' diverse identities and needs contribute to a Win-Win workplace, let's move into Chapter Four, where we'll consider the urgency and upside of reimagining employee benefits.

CHAPTER FOUR

REIMAGINING EMPLOYEE BENEFITS

At many times throughout your career, you've likely considered the importance of your employee benefits package. Maybe you've even made career decisions based on the package you're offered by a prospective employer. But have you ever been consulted about what should be part of the standard benefits package? How can a workplace truly address employee needs without consulting those employees?

Too often, not listening to employees leads to suboptimal outcomes, which, in turn, may manifest in the misallocation of resources and result in a Zero-Sum workplace. When employers fail to listen to the needs of their workers, values remain misaligned, and employees may have to focus on their own needs over the needs of the company. The benefits of a job should match the needs of the employees receiving those benefits.

This chapter expands on what was touched upon in Chapter Three: what a Win-Win workplace needs to do to make sure its benefits match its employees' interests. We'll look at how intersectional points are dynamic in nature in order to help you get a clearer picture of why employee benefits that are truly incentivizing require personalization and flexibility. And this personalization and flexibility can only be done economically at scale, with the use of technology.

Vickie's Story: *Managing Aging Parents and Work*

Vickie Braden, a seasoned marketing manager in the vibrant heart of Los Angeles, led a life of success with the freedom to revel in the independence of her singlehood. She described her days to me as a combination of creativity, autonomy, and deadlines. Until the plot of her life took an unforeseen twist.[1] Vickie's father, a cornerstone in her emotional architecture, suffered a stroke, and overnight she found herself a caregiver, responsible not only for her father's well-being but also for the formidable financial burden that accompanied it.

The once carefree drives through Los Angeles that Vickie enjoyed were transformed into a relentless pilgrimage, driving a hundred miles each way to a rehabilitation center. The toll was not just on her emotions but also on her finances. The road became her constant companion, each mile a lesson in sacrifice and determination.

During this challenging time, her employer emerged as an unexpected ally. An understanding boss recognized her need to be out of the office, and so Vickie was free to work from her father's rehabilitation center. A virtual private network (VPN) connection for her laptop was her bridge between the professional and the personal.

Yet, the strains were palpable, and during these months of remote work, Vickie discovered the limitations of the benefits her workplace offered. As a single woman without children, the standard childcare benefits were useless to her. But that was the only version of family-care benefits her company offered. Articulating her needs to her employer at such a vulnerable juncture felt like overwhelming. She was torn between navigating her full-time professional responsibilities and the personal responsibilities of her "second job" of family caregiving.

The strain led Vickie to look elsewhere, and she left for a new job that promised permanent flexibility in working hours and benefits tailored to the circumstances of her life. It was a new start with an organization that prioritized her well-being and upheld the Win-Win workplace pillars.

Vickie's story echoes the sentiments of countless others navigating the delicate balance between work and life. Her experience demonstrates the inadequacies of one-size-fits-all benefits in the evolving professional landscape.

One-size-fits-all employee benefits packages do not work for the same reason that one-size-fits-all shoes do not fit. Each employee has a different set of needs based on their present situation and concerns. When employers mandate that certain sums are allocated to earned programs, or to benefits that do not suit the employee, it can lead to frustration, disappointment, and, over time, an outdated and ineffective Zero-Sum workplace.

Certain employees may value childcare, while others may have a vested interest in access to medical care. Other employees place educational opportunities or autonomy in how they work above everything else. An equitable future of work in a Win-Win workplace must involve reimagining a system of employee benefits flexible enough to meet employees' needs but simple enough for employees to understand what they are getting, in relation to what they are giving up. A disconnect between the benefits offered and the benefits needed occurs not only for frontline workers but also for those in the C-suite. The answer to this problem lies in giving all employees the agency to partner with companies to optimize their individual benefit selections. Companies that have done this have seen an increase in employee satisfaction and an overall reduction in benefits costs. My research showed that companies that leverage the strategy of reimagining employee benefits in relation to paid vacation time or paid time off, sick leave, and maternity and paternity leave, saw an improvement in financial metrics including valuation, revenue, profits, and assets. Notably, backup dependent care stood out as having the most pronounced positive impact among the benefit variables.

Rachel's Story: *Navigating Parenthood and Leadership*

In the dynamic realm of education technology startups, Rachel Romer, the visionary CEO leading Guild Education, one of the largest players in the field, had a problem. In 2018, on the brink of welcoming twin girls into the world, she was orchestrating a groundbreaking $40 million Series C funding round.[2] Balancing the expectations of employees and investors—all under the watchful eyes of the business world—Rachel found herself facing a dilemma that transcended boardroom conversations and went to the very essence of her identity: how to navigate the uncharted waters of maternity leave as a young, first-time CEO.

Rachel's uncertainty wasn't merely a personal dilemma; it echoed broader narratives woven into the fabric of female leadership. She recalled a mentor's early return from maternity leave and subsequent struggle to balance family and career. Also weighing on Rachel was what kind of role model she would be to her twenty-something peers, what kind of answer she would be to the looming question of whether motherhood and a successful career were at all compatible.

Rachel couldn't escape the shadows cast by high-profile women leaders like Marissa Mayer, the former CEO of Yahoo! who chose a swift return to work after giving birth.[3] Mayer's well-publicized decision, seen as a reassurance to boards and investors, sparked debates about the expectations placed on female executives.

Admiration for Mayer's accomplishments were colored by envy and judgment, a mix of emotions with which Rachel herself grappled. Privileges afforded to Mayer because of her CEO title and socioeconomic status—like ample resources for nannies and remodeling the office for parenthood—were mere fantasy for most other working women. There was, for Rachel, an unspoken fear that Mayer had set an impossibly high bar that would become the new standard for female executives.

In the end, the mom-to-be chose transparency (pillar eight of the Win-Win workplace). Admitting that she had no predefined playbook for the company's working parents, Rachel communicated to entire team her that she would craft a new blueprint for the company's benefits that embraced choice and individuality.[4]

This commitment resonated with employees, especially considering the work they all did for Guild Education, which manages education assistance benefits for Fortune 500 firms by connecting employees with continuing education and offers benefit packages highly tailored to an individual's interests and circumstances.

In addition to what they did for their clients' employees, Guild invested in their own workers by opening a $1-million daycare center on their Denver-based company's campus in response to employees' concerns about childcare costs and quality.[5] This new center provided a critical service to their then 940 employees. As a result of this decision, Guild boasted an impressive 96 percent approval rate among parents during the pandemic. Now, Rachel is working alongside national nonprofits and legislators to create a step-by-step guide that helps other corporate leaders open on-site childcare at their firms.

The impact of Rachel's decision reverberated throughout the Guild organization, transforming it into a workplace that honored the diverse choices and needs of its people. The results were tangible: increased employee satisfaction, heightened loyalty, and a workplace culture that fostered creativity and collaboration. In short, a Win-Win workplace.

Leaders with Rachel's vision should evaluate even mainstream, highly valued benefits in response to employee voices in order to create a Win-Win workplace. When the CEO of a fast-casual restaurant offered employees a 401(k) plan, frontline workers voiced their concerns about immediate needs, including housing and transportation. The CEO changed the benefits package to allow more choice in the allocation of dollars to benefits that mattered most to employees, which gave them more control over their destinies. Guild became a case study for companies looking to redefine the intersection of career and family life. Rachel's story demonstrates the complexities of leadership and identity, as well as the delicate balance between personal and professional spheres. Her visionary leadership is a testament to breaking free from established norms, embracing transparency, and creating a workplace that not only attracts top talent but also champions the holistic well-being of its workforce.[6]

Let's now take a look at how one retailer centered employee voices to reimagine a benefit customization, aligning with the Win-Win process of change and creating a Win-Win workplace for employers and employees alike.

Case Study: *Tesco and Zeelo Solve the Commuting Dilemma*

In 2021, Tesco, a leading UK retailer, faced a significant challenge: attracting and retaining talent at their distribution centers due to limited public transportation options. As part of a strategy to center employee voices (pillar one of the Win-Win workplace), they conducted an employee listening survey and found

- 95.2 percent of employees reported that having access to a transportation benefit was important to them

- 90.7 of employees said they cannot get to work without a transportation service because of the timing of their shifts and lack of options.

To address this employee-identified problem, Tesco turned to its Red Door initiative, which invites innovators to offer ideas to improve Tesco's guest services and includes finding improvements in how the company serves its workers. Tesco partnered with Zeelo, a company that offers transportation solutions as an employee benefit in the United Kingdom and the United States. Shortly afterward, the retailer introduced a shuttle service that has proven popular with employees, good for the environment, *and* good for the bottom line.

TRANSPORTATION AS A BENEFIT

In 2024, I interviewed Sam Ryan, the cofounder of Zeelo, to learn more about the impacts of offering transportation as a benefit.[7] Sam shared with me that having grown up in rural Oxfordshire where everyone owned a vehicle, he and his team at Zeelo were acutely aware of the car dependency in cities outside major metropolitan areas like London. "When we looked at the data, we saw that in places like London and New York, about 80 percent of people use public transit, walk, or cycle to work. But in cities like Manchester, Birmingham, or Boston, 80 percent of people are car-dependent," Sam explained.

One of Sam's critical learnings from the COVID-19 pandemic was the increased responsibility employers took on to help their employees get to work. "Employers started to realize that helping their employees with transportation was essential for maintaining operations and filling jobs," Sam said. This shift in employer mindset was evident in Zeelo's partnership with Tesco. Tesco believed that by providing shuttle service as a benefit they could eliminate transportation as barrier to work. Tesco also believed that the benefit would help attract talent to fill open positions.

This partnership aimed to provide convenient and affordable bus routes for employees, thereby eliminating the need for personal vehicles for 81 percent of participating employees. Zeelo's service ran a route from the port city of Hull in East Yorkshire, England, to Tesco's distribution centers three times a day, covering all shift patterns. With a single ticket costing £2, workers saved an average of £10–20 per week. This initiative not only made commuting more accessible but also offered significant financial savings for Tesco's employees.

THE IMPACT ON EMPLOYEE SATISFACTION AND BUSINESS SUCCESS

Tesco has shared that the results of this partnership were transformative for their employees. As part of their employee listening strategy, they learned that employee satisfaction saw a marked improvement, with 94 percent of employees reporting better mental well-being at work. Additionally, 98 percent felt they were saving money on commuting, 92 percent felt they were saving time, and 72 percent expressed a greater willingness to stay with the company longer due solely to the transportation benefit. As part of the Red Door initiative, Tesco reported these findings to staff and gave permission to Zeelo to share these results publicly as a written case study, thereby using human-capital reporting as a competitive strategy (pillar eight of the Win-Win workplace).[8]

Michael Holmes, a distribution center manager at Tesco, highlighted the positive impact on recruitment and retention. Prior to implementing the Zeelo service, Tesco had unfilled positions at their distribution centers. Through offering transportation as a benefit, Tesco managed to recruit enough employees to meet their operational needs, which, as Holmes shared, "ensure[s] we fit our headcount, which means we can do the volume for stores."[9] From an environmental perspective, Zeelo's service had another substantial positive impact. In 2023 alone, the shuttle service's fully electric vehicles eliminated 64,000 car journeys, reducing CO_2 emissions by over 411 tons. This reduction contributed to Tesco's sustainability goals and demonstrated the broader benefits of the program.

CALCULATING TESCO'S RETURN ON INVESTMENT

The financial benefits for Tesco providing transportation as a benefit were also considerable. Tesco tracked key metrics before and after the transportation benefit offering, and the program showed a significant return on investment. Productivity losses due to unfilled vacancies were estimated at 55 percent; absenteeism costs at 0.5 percent; and recruitment costs, due to a high churn rate, were around 27 percent for one recruitment round, potentially doubling if two cycles were needed. The Zeelo shuttle service reduced churn by 70 percent, resulting in substantial savings in recruitment costs.[10]

Furthermore, the productivity improvement among employees using the service was estimated to yield 3 percent in savings. Additional savings included the cost of a transport manager (0.5 percent per year), CO_2 offsetting (0.07 percent per year), and rider payments (1.5 percent per year). The total value of the service in 2023 was estimated at mid-nine figures. Tesco estimates that the value of service will increase by 47 percent in one year, net of program costs.[11]

This case study demonstrates how forward-thinking companies can leverage technology and transportation solutions to create a positive impact on their employees' lives. By addressing transportation barriers, Tesco improved employee well-being, boosted recruitment and retention, and reduced their environmental footprint. The partnership with Zeelo serves as a powerful example of how innovative solutions can drive significant business and environmental benefits. We will discuss more about how to approach calculating return on investment in Chapter Ten.

WHAT THE RESEARCH SAYS

Our research examined data from 355 Fortune 500 companies and looked at a range of different benefits with a specific focus on caregiving needs. We found that offering a comprehensive benefits package that includes paid time off, paid parental leave (including maternity and paternity leave), subsidized childcare, and backup dependent care may lead to significant financial gains. Companies that provide robust benefits packages tend to see increased profits, revenue, and valuation. Supporting employees with benefits that help them manage personal and caregiving responsibilities can enhance their productivity, thus improving the company's financial health.

Companies that excel in reimagining employee benefits demonstrate strong financial performance, with 43 percent seeing growth in revenue, 54 percent in profits, 47 percent in assets, and 56 percent in valuation. This data highlights how investing in employee benefits not only improves employee well-being but also drives positive financial outcomes across key business metrics.

Process of Change: *Six Steps to Reimagining Benefits*

Prepare

1. **Identify opportunities to center employee voice:** Conduct surveys and focus groups to gather employee feedback on current benefits and identify areas for improvement. Analyze employee identities and understand their unique needs at different life stages. Just as Rachel Romer analyzed the diverse needs of Guild Education's employees, such as their concerns about childcare, use surveys and focus groups to understand the specific requirements of your workforce. For

example, consider life stages and unique circumstances like parenthood, mental health needs, or financial stability.

Act

2. **Reimagine benefits:** Based on employee feedback, brainstorm innovative benefit offerings. Consider benefits such as housing (e.g., security deposit or down-payment assistance), mental health resources, eldercare support, and student loan repayment assistance. Consider flexible work arrangements, expanded parental leave, subsidized childcare, or wellness programs. Recall how Romer invested in on-site childcare as a benefit to meet the needs of parents, providing them with peace of mind by allowing working parents to be in close proximity to their children.

Refine

3. **Engage with employees to develop new approaches to Win-Win working relationships:** Present the proposed benefit options to employees and solicit their feedback. This fosters a sense of ownership and increases the likelihood of adoption. For instance, Guild Education's decision to open a daycare center was based on employee feedback and concerns about childcare costs and quality.

4. **Evaluate outcomes and adoption of the new approaches:** Gather feedback from employees on the effectiveness of the changes. Track the effectiveness of the new benefits. Monitor employee satisfaction, engagement, productivity, and cost-effectiveness. Like Tesco saw a significant reduction in employee churn by 70 percent, improved productivity yielding a substantial increase in overall savings, and a positive return on investment, indicating that the new transportation benefits had a profound impact on their workforce

and operational efficiency. Similarly, Guild Education saw an impressive 96 percent approval rate among parents during the pandemic. Use metrics to assess the impact of the benefits offered.

5. **Adjust the new approaches as needed:** Be prepared to adapt your approach based on the evaluation results. Refine and iterate on your benefits based on employee feedback and program outcomes. The iterative process should mirror Romer's approach of continuously improving benefits to meet evolving employee needs.

Communicate and Learn

6. **Keep your employees informed throughout the process:** Share the results of your evaluation and encourage ongoing feedback. This fosters a culture of continuous improvement in your benefits program. Transparency, as demonstrated by Romer's open communication about her maternity leave and new benefit initiatives, helps build trust and engagement among employees. Similarly, Tesco's commitment to publicly innovate in order to improve both employee experience and customer services through its Red Door initiative showcases the importance of ongoing transparency and communication.

THE SIGNIFICANCE OF REIMAGINING BENEFITS

Vickie's dilemma and Rachel's bold decision paint a clear picture of the limitations of one-size-fits-all benefits in today's diverse workforce. We have discussed how employees have varied needs based on their identities (Chapter Three). While it may seem easier to follow a one-size-fits-all approach, personalization, when leveraged intentionally and responsibly, can help managers and companies alike to meaningfully serve the individual employee and, en masse, create a transformative workforce, a Win-Win workforce.

So, let us step into this future with open hearts and curious minds, ready to embrace the transformative potential of reimagined benefits, crafted not just for individuals but for the collective well-being of the workforce. As the curtain rises on this new chapter in the history of work, the possibilities are boundless, and the potential for positive change immeasurable.

By showing a willingness to reimagine the perks of employment, companies can create a future of work where employee benefits are woven from the unique threads of each individual's needs and aspirations, making the Win-Win workplace the norm. As an employee you can introduce companies like Zeelo to your manager and to human resources. Remember, leveraging your position to partner with leadership is a way to leverage your own voice within the workplace. Tailored benefits that people actually want can lead to a more satisfied, productive, and healthier workforce and benefit everyone in the company. In Chapter Five, we'll explore how a specific subset of employees within an organization—frontline managers—can help a company further evolve into a Win-Win workplace.

CHAPTER FIVE

ACTIVATING FRONTLINE LEADERS

Y ou almost certainly know the term "middle manager." It's often spoken with a knowing eye roll or a snicker, the inside joke being that middle managers are powerless paper pushers, bureaucrats, defenders of the status quo, and, as *Harvard Business Review* cataloged their bad rap, the very definition of mediocrity.[1] The *New York Times* columnist David Brooks put it this way: "Nobody writes poems about middle managers."[2]

But it's time we start (metaphorically, of course).

Better yet, let's call these misunderstood but pivotal people in the workplace what they really are—frontline leaders or frontline managers (I will use these terms interchangeably)—and give them empowering new training and listening protocols so that they can unlock their full potential to create a Win-Win workplace, both for the workers they supervise on the organization's front lines and for the executives back at headquarters measuring success.

Frontline leaders are *key* to the cyclical Win-Win process of change and building a Win-Win workplace. But in today's workplaces, they are often ill-equipped, preoccupied with self-preservation, and hampered by burnout. Outmoded work paradigms and mental models, deeply ingrained assumptions, and generalizations that shape our understanding and actions don't help matters. To successfully achieve Win-Win workplace goals, organizational leaders must understand these challenges and develop new policies to help frontline managers navigate around obstacles.

FIRSTHAND EXPERIENCE: THE PETER PRINCIPLE

My own experience as a frontline leader shapes my perspective on the Win-Win workplace. From one of my earliest management positions, I can still picture a direct report, Laura, telling me—for the third time in as many weeks—that she would not be able to deliver a project on the timeline I expected. My response, out of frustration, was to question her commitment to the organization and to her own career. Her eyes narrowed while her forehead creased. Laura replied that she was committed to the job, but as an independent parent she was unable to work extra hours like I did. She was responsible for her eight-year-old daughter who needed her. My face fell as the truth hit me: what I saw as an unwillingness to do whatever it took to get the job done was, in fact, a mother struggling to balance the demands on her at home with the expectations of a no-excuses manager at work. Before that moment, I had no idea of Laura's lived realities. I saw her solely as an associate in marketing. I didn't see the fullness of who she was and all the weight she carried. That hit me in the gut. When our conversation that day forced me to stop and think about her in full, I obviously could not say—could never say—that my project deadlines were more important than the little human in her care at home.

This was my first hard lesson being a frontline manager: the power of empathy and human connection, and the need for leadership training. I was disappointed in myself and felt like a failure. According to the data, I wasn't alone. Frontline leaders directly supervise up to 80 percent of the workforce in many organizations, and commonly cited research suggests that 50–60 percent of these managers fail within their first one to two years.[3]

I was twenty-three years old when I was first made a manager. I was promoted because I was good at my job as a sales coordinator, not because I was a good leader of people. As a sales coordinator, I was an individual contributor. My managers assigned me a task and I was consistent at getting it done on time and being a problem solver who anticipated challenges and roadblocks, and alerted managers well in advance. That stuff came easily to me. And I was ambitious. Later, I would describe my style as Type A. I knew I could perform well individually and accomplish any task needed. But to be a manager? I wasn't long out of college and the only thing I knew about managers was what I had seen in movies and experienced in the part-time and entry-level jobs I did to put myself through school. My bosses were more like the boss character in *Swimming with Sharks*. That 1994 movie satirized the cutthroat entertainment industry, explored how far a bad boss can push an ambitious young underling, and portrayed the toll such a toxic work environment can take on an individual. All of this is to say that I had very low expectations of my managers and didn't know what a good manager looked like. Behind my own ambition and Type A personality was plain old fear: I didn't want to let my managers down and risk being fired. So, I never pushed back on anything they asked of me. I *acted* positive even as my world was falling apart.

I was thousands of dollars in debt with student loans and no parental safety net to help me. I just put my head down, did my work, and silently suffered. I had grown up, professionally, to believe that you're at work to do your job and your boss is there to do their job, not mentor you or invest in you. Their contribution was giving me the job in the first place. It was on me to perform in a way that was pleasing to them and to contribute to the company's success, regardless of how my manager treated me.

Fast forward to how I performed as a manager: I had codified my experience as an individual contributor into what I expected from the people who reported to me. I had been a no-excuses top performer, a consistent contributor. I expected the same from my direct reports. After all, if they turned in a poor performance, it would reflect poorly on me. I was the quintessential bad manager. But how could I have been a good one without any training or mentoring in the role? What I am describing is what Laurence J. Peter coined in 1969 as the Peter Principle, which suggests that if organizations consistently prioritize promoting their top performers within their current roles, they may eventually find themselves elevating individuals beyond their optimal capacity, ultimately diminishing their effectiveness in those roles and—worse yet—diminishing the success of the company as a whole.

THE WIN-WIN VALUE PROPOSITION

I often say to my clients, "Managing people is the job that you don't get appropriately compensated for." Does this sound familiar? If you have ever been a manager, you have probably felt or thought this at some point. Frontline managers constantly pivot between their roles as leader, subordinate, and individual contributor. A staggering 82 percent of new managers in the United Kingdom are what the Chartered Management Institute calls "accidental managers" who were promoted because they had been great individual contributors, not because they showed signs of being great managers.[4]

This is why it is imperative that organizations and managers alike buy into the value of a Win-Win workplace. The frontline managers of an organization are pivotal to employee satisfaction and retention of talent. The reality is that poor leadership of one's direct manager is one of the top reasons people leave their jobs. But when these managers adopt a Win-Win workplace approach, they can transform into frontline leaders and can significantly boost employee retention by fostering an environment where everyone feels valued and engaged and where employees are more likely to stay and excel.[5]

Leaders who are genuinely committed to both the company's goals and their team's well-being build trust and loyalty. This kind of commitment helps employees feel more connected to the organization's mission, reducing their desire to leave. These frontline leaders who align their focus on their team's well-being with the company's objectives transform the Win-Win workplace approach from a strategy into a lived reality, boosting overall performance and success.[6]

This role of frontline leader transcends a new title or pay raise. It's a mindset shift. Managers who step up to the role of frontline leader are now cultural carriers for the Win-Win workplace culture, a serious responsibility for championing organizational values, adapting an ownership mindset, and boosting inclusion.

Lisen Stromberg, founder of PrismWork, an organization that conducts corporate culture research and assessments, wanted to understand the frontline leader's lived experience in the workplace—and especially their role in inclusion and DEI initiatives—when she surveyed 2,246 US professional men for PrismWork's 2023 RESET report.[7] Why just men? "Because they are an essential piece of the diversity, equity, and inclusion puzzle," Stromberg and her team wrote in their report. "Men have much to gain by building and supporting strong working relationships in their organizations, and the world has much to gain by having them engaged in DEI."[8] And, let's face it: men hold 60 percent of the management positions in American business and globally this number jumps to 67.8 percent.[9] The survey showed that men who identified as managers were struggling. "The men were begging for guidance from their companies and specifically from the CEO and the HR team and were stymied because they weren't getting the training they need to get out of zero-sum thinking," Stromberg told me over lunch.[10]

In addition to basic management training, frontline managers need to understand the Win-Win process of change and the support resources and incentives they need to get the process rolling. Investment in support for frontline leaders—through management training, resources, and incentives—benefits the entire workforce *and* the bottom line. Let's explore each category in more detail.

MANAGEMENT TRAINING

- **Win for frontline leader:** Training programs equip frontline leaders with the skills to champion values, foster ownership, and create an inclusive environment. This leads to a more engaged and productive workforce.
- **Win for employees:** Employees enjoy better leadership and feel supported in their professional development.

SUPPORT RESOURCES

- **Win for frontline leader:** Leaders get resources, including communication tools, templates, and access to human resources support, which makes it easier for them to implement Win-Win changes. They can also access other great services, such as Empower Work, which provides a twenty-four-hour line for employees and managers alike to call for any personal work-related issue.[11] Even the best manager will not have all the answers, and a service like Empower Work allows them to be a resource for their direct reports.

- **Win for employees:** Employees have access to the tools and support they need to succeed and thrive within the company culture.

INCENTIVES

- **Win for frontline leaders:** Frontline leaders who excel at embracing the Win-Win process of change and building a Win-Win workplace get rewards and recognition, which reinforces the desired behavior. This could include bonuses, increased responsibility, or public recognition.
- **Win for employees:** Employees see that these behaviors are valued by the company, which can boost morale and engagement. Additionally, some incentive programs can directly benefit employees, such as team-based rewards for achieving inclusion goals.
- **A Win-Win environment motivates everyone** to contribute to a positive and successful workplace.

CHAMPIONING THE ORGANIZATIONAL VALUES

My experience working *on* the front line and *with* frontline managers highlights the need for targeted support for this crucial leadership group. Frontline managers bridge the gap between senior leadership and the front line (both the workers and customers there), playing a vital role in employee engagement, performance, and overall organizational success. Effective frontline managers must actively promote and embody the core principles of their organization. It's not enough for them to know the values; they must live them through the following actions:

- **Lead by example:** They consistently demonstrate the company's values in their actions and decisions.

- **Educate and inspire others:** They help colleagues understand the values and how they apply to daily work.
- **Hold others accountable:** They gently remind people when their behaviors stray from the values, fostering a positive and aligned culture.

OWNERSHIP MINDSET

An employee or manager with an ownership mindset takes initiative and responsibility for their work and its outcomes. They go beyond simply completing tasks and strive for excellence. A person with an ownership mindset has the following attributes:

- **Proactive problem-solver:** They identify and address issues before they become major problems.
- **Takes initiative:** They don't wait to be told what to do; they see opportunities and take action.
- **Accountability:** They take ownership of their mistakes and learn from them.
- **Results-oriented:** They focus on achieving goals and delivering high-quality work.

INCLUSION BOOSTER

An "inclusion booster" is someone who actively creates a welcoming and supportive environment for all. They go beyond tolerance and work to ensure all voices are heard and valued. An inclusion booster has the following attributes:

- **Celebrates diversity:** They recognize and appreciate the unique skills and perspectives everyone brings to the table.
- **Promotes respect:** They foster a culture where everyone feels comfortable sharing their ideas and opinions.

- **Challenges bias:** They identify and address unconscious bias that might hinder inclusion;
- **Builds bridges:** They connect people from different backgrounds and help them understand each other.

GLOBAL PEOPLE LEADERS

To see exactly how managers can be successfully activated, let's look inside the programs and policies of three large brand-name financial and retail institutions that collectively have billions of dollars in assets, hundreds of thousands of employees, and tens of thousands of frontline managers. These businesses' senior leaders in human resources roles spoke with me in depth about their management training on the condition that I present our discussions as an anonymized composite.[12]

For the sake of clarity and brevity, I'll give my interview subjects a single composite name: Global People Leaders (GPLs). The upper management of these organizations recognizes how critical manager effectiveness is in driving employee experience and customer satisfaction, the GPLs told me in interviews. And they are taking action.

In today's competitive landscape, highly engaged employees—as measured by the strong mental and emotional connection to the organization that they work for, their team, and their work—are the backbone of a positive work environment, directly translating to better customer service.[13]

Engaged employees are doing more than just showing up for a paycheck. They take initiative, go the extra mile for customers, and are passionate about what they do because they believe in the company's mission. Engaged employees are more likely to

- be friendly and helpful to customers;
- proactively solve problems; and
- go the extra mile to exceed customer expectations.

Having a happy and engaged workforce is a Win-Win for both the company and the customer.

Empowering Frontline Leaders, Transforming Customer Experience

Gallup recently found that managers are responsible for about 70 percent of the differences in employee engagement within different parts of a company.[14] This means that whether employees feel motivated, committed, and satisfied with their jobs largely depends on their managers. In turn, this means managers play a huge role in influencing performance.

The GPLs I spoke with in the tech, healthcare, and retail sectors collectively support tens of thousands of frontline managers across the United States. One of the GPLs succinctly summarized the problem when it comes to managers: "We know that we have a frontline manager problem. We have heard it from employees that report to them. What we are trying to do is operationalize the insights across thousands of managers. It is no small task."

Individual managers and supervisors are pivotal in managing people, overseeing teams, implementing policies, fostering engagement, and ensuring compliance, significantly shaping overall management effectiveness. Uneven frontline management directly impacts the bottom line by causing operational inefficiencies, lower productivity, increased turnover, and reduced profitability. Consistent frontline management is essential for operational excellence, high employee morale, and achieving financial objectives. Simply put, an institution's effectiveness often hinges on its least effective manager.

The GPLs I spoke with shared that innovative strategies like using manager effectiveness metrics are crucial because they enable data-driven decision-making, enhance performance, improve employee experience, inform targeted development programs, increase retention and engagement, align managers with organizational goals, and support continuous improvement. By centering employee voices, these Win-Win GPLs were leveraging pillar one of the Win-Win workplace. They listened to their employees' sentiments and then used data analytics to identify specific areas for improvement and tailor individual manager-development programs. Crucial to this strategy is the effective use of the following management tools:

- **Regular pulse surveys:** The GPLs conduct targeted pulse surveys tailored to specific business lines and employee segments. They include a regular set of questions around employee engagement and interactions with managers and ratings in response to statements such as "I would recommend my manager to another colleague."
- **Performance reviews with manager capabilities assessment:** Manager performance reviews include an assessment of their capabilities, providing valuable data on leadership strengths and weaknesses.

After collecting data from these various sources, the firms used generative AI to assist with the analysis of hundreds of thousands of data points. It is through this analysis that these GPLs and their companies gain a comprehensive understanding of employee sentiment toward their managers nationwide in the United States and globally.

Similarly, data gathered through the centering-employee strategies discussed in Chapter One can identify trends and patterns in manager effectiveness. Based on this analysis, the companies that I studied across the 355 created targeted development programs for different manager segments:

- **High performers:** Recognition programs and opportunities for knowledge sharing are implemented to leverage their strengths and foster a culture of mentorship.
- **Medium performers:** Coaching and mentoring programs are implemented to address specific areas for improvement.
- **Low performers:** Personalized development plans with automated professional development plans and facilitated discussions with human resources partners are provided to support significant improvement.

This data-driven approach has yielded positive results. According to the GPLs, their firms have seen a demonstrable improvement in manager effectiveness, leading to a more engaged workforce. Additionally, the companies have observed a direct correlation between manager effectiveness and customer satisfaction. They emphasized this connection, with one stating, "We have evidence that shows a correlation between good frontline management and a decrease of customer complaints. We have also seen that the frontline manager has an impact on higher sales." This translates into a significant financial impact, with the GPLs estimating a potential return on investment that goes into the multi-millions of dollars.[15]

The success of the data-driven employee listening makes it a key part of any employer's frontline manager strategy. By focusing on manager development, the successful frontline leaders we followed fostered positive work environments, which is directly linked to business success.

Key Takeaways

- Publish a well-defined "effective manager" profile to precisely identify development needs.

- Develop a comprehensive training program for all newly promoted and newly hired leaders, ensuring they fully understand their role expectations and the key indicators of success.
- Continuously gather and analyze detailed feedback from various aspects of employees' experiences to inform strategic human resources decisions.
- Tailor manager development programs based on employee insights to enhance both employee experience and business performance.
- Leverage new technology like generative AI and machine learning to assist with analysis and understand the impact on business operations.
- Share best practices and learnings both internally and externally (as we will detail in Chapter Eight) to foster a culture of data-driven talent development within the industry.

EMERGING FOCUS ON TRAINING FRONTLINE LEADERS

Whether facilitating change management or advancing business goals, managers are on the front lines of employee engagement, performance, and retention. To stay agile and ready in a constantly changing environment, managers need training support and the right tools as their job is evolving. These frontline leaders are 46 percent less satisfied with their jobs than senior executives (those who manage at least fifteen people).[16] They have also struggled more than twice as much as executives when it comes to maintaining a sense of belonging, according to a survey from Future Forum, a consortium partnered with Slack alongside Boston Consulting Group, MillerKnoll, and Management Leadership for Tomorrow.[17] The group surveyed 9,032 knowledge workers who identify as "skilled office workers" across the United States, and other countries, over three years to understand how their perceptions and challenges in the workplace have evolved.[18]

As organizations move toward more flexible work schedules and digital communication, frontline managers roles are evolving from paper-pushing attendance checkers to facilitators of a work environment where people are inspired to do their best work. This shift requires embracing digital tools for tracking and aligning teams while promoting a "default-to-open" culture that enhances collaboration and decision-making across distributed teams.[19]

Remember Genevieve Richards, the manager featured in Chapter Three? Her job was to enforce company policy for her direct reports. Fortunately, she took a strong interest in her employees, learning their strengths, weaknesses, habits, and lived realities. Unfortunately, the company restricted her from being the empathetic and flexible manager she wanted to be. Believing that understanding her team was crucial to good management, she made it a priority to address issues directly with her team before taking administrative action. Her close proximity to her workers gave her valuable insight into each one's work style. Unfortunately, the company failed to recognize and support this approach.

WHAT OTHER COMPANIES ARE DOING FOR FRONTLINE MANAGERS

In November 2022, I participated in a conversation hosted by The 19th, a nonprofit, independent news organization based in Austin, Texas, to dig into the challenges faced by managers in the "new normal" work environment. The discussion was joined by executives from Slack, H-E-B, and Dell who shared what was happening on their front lines and how their companies are specifically supporting frontline leaders.[20] The key takeaways are instructive more broadly:

- **Combatting stress and burnout:** Christina Janzer, Slack's senior vice president of research and analysis, explained how her department keeps a finger on the pulse of managers by running a quarterly survey of more than 10,000 desk workers around the world. Their most recent findings (October 2022) show frontline leaders experiencing 40 percent more work-related stress and anxiety—and a 43 percent spike in burnout—over the previous year. This can lead to reverting to outdated management styles, she noted. One finding that surprised her: flexible work policies—"both for where you work and also for when"—led to improved productivity and were cited as the number-one factor in improving company culture.

- **Active listening and support:** Organizations need to prioritize listening to their managers' needs and offering solutions. Vanice Hayes, Dell Technologies' chief culture, diversity, and inclusion officer, said that in addition to seeking employee feedback on an annual basis (Dell has 130,000 "team members" globally), the company does "regular, frequent check-ins." Questions in those sessions go much deeper than how employees are completing tasks to "How are they doing as people? How can I help? Are they feeling overwhelmed? What do they want to do next?" said Hayes. "We are asking our leaders to know everyone, really know their talent and understand people's aspirations and skills. . . . They want to be valued. They want to be seen. And so, whatever we can do as leaders to facilitate that, that's what we have to continue to focus on."

- **Data-driven development:** Data is key to understanding the evolving skills and experiences of frontline managers. This allows companies to tailor development opportunities and prevent valued employees from leaving.

- **Employee-centric solutions:** Flexible scheduling and dedicated focus time can significantly boost productivity and creativity for overloaded managers who wear many hats. Slack, for example, approaches schedule flexibility at the team level, where they "com[e] up with agreements for how we're going to collaborate and when," said Janzer. "We have things like core collaboration hours which, for some teams are like 10 a.m. to 1 p.m. These are the hours you're expected to work, but everything else is flexible." Slack has also experimented with focus time—and eliminating as many meetings as possible. Every quarter, two weeks are carved out as "maker weeks." These are no-meeting weeks where people are able to focus and have more creative time. "Data that we collect afterwards says people love these weeks because they are able to get so much more work done," said Janzer.

These are just some examples, and the specific strategies will vary by company. However, the key takeaway is that companies that prioritize supporting their frontline managers through targeted initiatives are more likely to retain valuable talent and foster a thriving work environment.

BECOMING A WIN-WIN LEADER

So, what is a Win-Win mentality, and what characteristics identify a Win-Win leader? In Stephen Covey's *The 7 Habits of Highly Effective People: Powerful Lessons in Personal Change*, he talks about the "Win/Win Mindset"—one that seeks mutual benefit.[21] By adopting the Win-Win mindset, Covey argues, you can build stronger relationships, achieve better results, and create a more positive and collaborative environment.

Everyone has the potential to develop a Win-Win mindset, but not everyone will become a Win-Win leader. Why? Some may simply not be interested in taking on the role. Some people—in fact, many people—enjoy being individual contributors and are still valuable to the organization as long as they embody a Win-Win mentality. Being a Win-Win leader is much more than being promoted to manager because you are an outstanding individual contributor. Managers who get the job that way are managers in name only. In the Win-Win workplace, individual contributors who demonstrate a Win-Win mindset are intentionally developed into Win-Win managers. The next step is that they make a commitment to becoming a Win-Win leader, which includes:

1. Prioritizing the growth and well-being of their team.

2. Creating a safe space for open communication and honest feedback.

3. Learning alongside their team and actively seeking opportunities for improvement.

4. Empowering others through mentorship and knowledge sharing.

5. Fostering a culture of trust, collaboration, and psychological safety.

When deciding to promote someone to a position managing people based on their performance, ensure that they have also demonstrated these qualities. Remember, this is just the prerequisite; it must be followed by orientation and ongoing training.

Building effective leaders requires continuous learning and development. Recognizing this need, my colleagues at Future Forward Strategies, the labor-market analytics and strategies firm I founded, introduced the Win-Win People Leader Training. This comprehensive program, based on the Win-Win process of

WHAT THE RESEARCH SAYS

This strategy empowers frontline leaders to champion initiatives promoting intersectionality and DEI in the workplace. While companies that hire a higher percentage of entry-level workers may experience higher turnover initially due to lower levels of experience, effectively supporting and training these new hires can foster loyalty and reduce attrition in the long run. In analyzing the 355 companies in our study, we observed a neutral effect on revenue and stock price. The limited number of companies implementing these strategies suggests that a larger sample is needed for deeper insights, presenting an opportunity for further research as these practices become more widely adopted.

According to the results of a 2022 leadership development survey published in *Training* magazine, nine out of ten top organizations that match their training programs to the preferences of newly promoted leaders see more success in developing their leadership skills.[22] A significant gap exists between high- and low-performing organizations: the former are 48 percent more likely to invest in new leaders through coaching and increased responsibility.[23]

change, is designed to cultivate leaders who not only excel in their roles but also prioritize the well-being and growth of their team members.[24] By offering a structured approach that operates year-round, we ensure that leaders have ongoing opportunities to enhance their skills, deepen their understanding, and adapt to evolving workplace dynamics. The following six-step plan serves as a road map for business leaders and frankly anyone included in hiring processes wanting to nurture a culture of continuous improvement and Win-Win relationships within their organization.

Process of Change: *Six Steps to Supporting Frontline Leaders*

Prepare

1. **Identify opportunities to center employee voices in the selection and professional development of frontline leaders:** When a potential frontline leader is identified for promotion or hire, ask about their leadership history and experience. When conducting reference checks, in addition to speaking to their management, ask to speak to one or two of their direct reports. (If they haven't had direct reports, ask to speak to a peer they collaborated with on a team project. This will help you understand how they lead upward, downward, and laterally, across teams). Make an analysis of where the frontline leader is in relation to the identified good managers on your team to begin to develop a training program based on the frontline leaders' goals and business needs.

Act

2. **Define core competencies and set up frontline leader onboarding:** Onboarding training should align with the case study of the GPLs, which, in turn, aligns with industry best practices, as 48 percent of top-performing companies provide new frontline leader training.[25] Create a core competencies framework to define essential skills and knowledge for frontline leaders. Design a comprehensive training program specifically for managers. Integrate data analytics to track and measure outcomes tied to business objectives. (We will discuss this further in Chapter Eight.) Explore the potential of AI and machine learning to personalize the learning experience for managers and translate quantitative and qualitative

data into actionable insights for improving manager training outcomes. A well-trained leadership team fosters a more positive and productive work environment for all employees, creating a Win-Win situation for the organization.

Refine

3. **Engage with employees to develop new approaches to support frontline leaders:** One human resources professional shared with me that their managers felt unsure how to address employee concerns like return-to-work anxiety. She also mentioned that spotting signs of distress in a remote workforce posed a challenge. Her point was that we are demanding more of our frontline managers than ever, and they need training. Based on the feedback received from their managers, this company implemented basic mental health awareness training for managers, which was incredibly well received. She shared with me that they were quite surprised by the huge appetite for this training. Following the training, the company engaged managers in listening tours, and managers felt more equipped with the language and vocabulary to discuss mental health.[26]

4. **Evaluate outcomes and adoption of the new approaches:** To assess a frontline leader program's impact on employees, we need a two-pronged approach. First, track adoption: Are frontline leaders actively using the new skills? Data and feedback can guide us, but observing their behavior—championing values, fostering ownership—reveals true integration. Second, we measure outcomes. Are employee engagement and team performance metrics improving? Go on a listening tour. Ask managers and their direct reports how training can be improved. And then act on their suggestions.

5. **Adjust the new approaches as needed:** Win-Win work-places require constant learning. Equip frontline leaders with the latest skills through micro-learning modules informed by direct-report, employee, peer, and manager feedback. This keeps learning relevant and addresses current needs. It's a Win-Win: frontline leaders learn the latest managements skills conveniently and hone their expertise, while the organization benefits from a skilled and engaged workforce, leading to improved performance. Invest in continuous learning and building a thriving workplace.

Communicate and Learn

6. **Communicate progress and learnings from implementing the new approaches:** Use short, bite-sized communication opportunities such as videos, articles, and podcasts to target managers and share progress. Disseminate best practices and learnings with other organizations to foster a culture of data-driven talent development within the industry. Think back to the examples of the leaders from Dell, H-E-B, and Slack who generously share best practices and learnings publicly, demonstrating their commitment to frontline managers and their people.

Status quo management skills like communication, conflict resolution, team empowerment, and emotional intelligence are important for any effective manager. The key differentiation of a frontline leader is an underlying Win-Win mindset, that the manager is focused on mutual benefits for themselves, their team, and the company when leveraging their skills in service of the organization fostering collective success.

Workplace transformation often fails because frontline management is overlooked and overwhelmed. In the Win-Win workplace, managers are no longer squeezed but stretched to reach their highest potential and become the engines of growth for the company. They willingly make the commitment to become Win-Win leaders driving workforce transformation, and they embrace their critical role in it. In a Win-Win workplace, frontline management is treated as a prized and critical role, and companies commit to supporting frontline managers with the training, resources, and compensation commensurate with both their contributions and potential.

In this chapter, we learned how to unlock the true potential of these frontline leaders while supporting them to become "engines of growth" and culture carriers who embody and promote an organization's core values, influencing others to align with its culture. What is the biggest barrier beyond training? The answer might surprise you. It's how we fundamentally view talent and qualifications altogether. Next, we will turn to Chapter Six to discuss how Win-Win workplaces rethink credentials.

CHAPTER SIX

RETHINKING CREDENTIALS

A Taco Bell cashier, a gas station attendant, a dog trainer, and a theoretical physicist walk into a bar . . .

The unlikely foursome was out celebrating a project they had just completed—right on deadline—for a Fortune 100 company that was readying a piece of wearable technology for release. "You saved this product," the company project manager gushed. "You saved my bonus!" In fact, this foursome of contract apprentices from the tech-talent firm Catalyte proved to be three times as productive and faster than the Fortune 100 company's in-house teams. The grateful and intrigued project manager asked what each of them did in their previous jobs. Catalyte founder and executive chairman Mike Rosenbaum, who spoke with me at length for this book in February 2023, enjoys sharing what happened next: "Folks went around the room and said, 'I used to work at a gas station. I worked at Taco Bell. I have a PhD in theoretical physics. I raised dogs to chase geese off a lake.' The project manager paused for a second. She had such deeply embedded assumptions about what excellence looks like, and our teams didn't reflect what she had in her head. She realized that her assumption was wrong." Rosenbaum remembers it well. "That was an incredibly rewarding moment."[1]

That project manager's aha moment is exactly what we need—writ large—to build the Win-Win workplace of the future. We need for employers and their hiring managers to rethink traditional credentials—graduation from a top university (bonus points for the Ivy League), experience at big-name companies—and access a bigger and better candidate pool by embracing diversity and inclusion. Let's face it: credentials on a résumé can look impressive, but they don't really say anything about whether the individual is equipped to do the job. Yet, we see companies throwing big money at the graduates coming out of the Ivy League, Stanford, and other big-name schools, leaving millions of people with unfinished degrees or no degrees completely overlooked. The competition for this limited pool of pedigreed candidates drives up their compensation. Demand begets scarcity. A premium is paid. As Mike, who is also an Oxford-trained economist with a Harvard law degree, quips, hiring managers are just "trying to read the tea leaves," which does not make for a great hiring strategy.

A brand name does not equal ability, potential, work ethic, experience, curiosity, or knowledge. An aptitude test someone took when they were seventeen should not forever dictate their future course of employment and economic mobility. In the research that led to his founding of Catalyte, Mike found that the traditional credentials most used in hiring correlate with a job candidate's socioeconomic background. This approach leaves an immense number of people in the United States undervalued by a labor market that relies on credentials and perpetuates the proliferation of Zero-Sum workplaces. Rethinking these old-school credentials and finding more accurate, more modern metrics to evaluate potential candidates is essential for business leadership in the future of work.

Starting with a new mindset for talent acquisition, Mike began hiring STARs, or those **S**killed **T**hrough **A**lternative **R**outes, a term coined by the nonprofit Opportunity@Work.[2] Mike explained to me:

> *If a third of the US is somehow undervalued in this way, you've got 100 million people. So, if 2 percent of that 100 million people—and there's probably more than that—are brilliant, you're talking about millions of people who are exceptional and don't have the appropriate pathways into the roles where they can thrive better than anyone else in that job. And so, if you can figure out who that person is, and break down those barriers to give that individual the pathway to be in the job where they will thrive, you can unleash massive amounts of economic power.*

In Chapter Five, we learned how frontline leaders can be incentivized to see the business imperative to run a Win-Win workplace. In this chapter, we shift our focus to what hiring managers need to do. We'll look at the concept of hiring for skills and explore case studies of companies that are using generative AI and machine learning solutions to expand their talent book, find more perfect matches, and save their recruitment dollars by identifying talent from within.

STARS: THE CATALYST FOR CATALYTE

Mike Rosenbaum would go on to found two venture-backed companies, leveraging non-degreed talent along the way. For over a decade, Mike's latest company, Catalyte, has used its predictive platform to identify non-degreed individuals with an aptitude for software development using logic tests. They then train these developers and offer them to top companies as on-demand talent.

Because Catalyte is focused on overlooked talent, it does not have to compete with companies placing computer science graduates. Overlooked talent is more market accessible and hirable at more competitive salaries. Plus, Catalyte has found that their non-degreed workforce is 40 percent more productive than their college-degreed counterparts and stays 25 percent longer at their company compared with the industry average.

Many big names have already taken notice of the STARs among us. Organizations like Accenture, Chevron, Cognizant, Google, Jobcase, LinkedIn, McKinsey & Company, Walmart, and Workday have joined what's called the "Tear the Paper Ceiling" campaign dedicated to hiring STARs.[3] Beyond the movement away from hiring based on college degrees, there is a broader shift in the philosophy underlying the creation and retention of human capital for many companies and organizations. The focus is now on the *skill*, not the job description. Companies are focusing on the skills required to execute their projects. They're rejecting the myth that low-wage means low-skill.[4]

EXCEEDING EXPECTATIONS BY ELIMINATING BIAS

You know that tried-and-true feel-good movie plot where the rag-tag group of misfits comes together and, against all odds, wins the big game against the rival school with kids that all look like they play professionally? All that team of misfits needed to win was guidance, a coach who believed in them, and camaraderie. Their coach may have started out frustrated, but before the movie's climax, she realizes that she has a team full of STARs. Cue the montage showing the team getting better every day. Hiring teams also need to recognize when they have a STAR on their hands.

STARs account for 70 million people in the workforce.[5] They are the 50 percent of the workforce that developed valuable skills through military service, community college, partial completion of a four-year degree, training programs, or, most commonly, through on-the-job experience.[6] That's exactly what STARs initiatives champion: reconceptualizing what an "A-Team" looks like.

This is important because you will not find diversity of experience and thought in a team full of graduates from the same schools, with the same backgrounds, who are now seeking the same lives.

They make movies about that, too. Usually, the theme is competition and dysfunction: the one least corrupted by the lust for power is the last one standing. Or the one person from a different background outmaneuvers the homogenous bunch to emerge victorious. These movies are not feel-good romps, and they definitely do not end with a triumphant scene where the community rushes the field, hoisting the team of winners into the air, a town united in glory. They are instead stories that focus on individual achievement rather than a team of underdogs who make good.

When employers rely on traditional, credentials-based hiring processes, the underdogs never get to take the field. The problem with the traditional hiring process is that focusing on credentials creates barriers for talented people who have acquired valuable skills or experience through alternative paths, such as apprenticeships, on-the-job training, or self-directed learning. Hiring managers may manifest bias by favoring applicants who they perceive are similar to themselves in background and experience, like when they give a job to a person from the same fraternity over another qualified individual.

Assuming that a four-year degree is sufficient can result in a poor fit between candidate and role, resulting in decreased productivity, increased turnover, and, ultimately, higher costs for the organization. All things being equal, degree holders in middle-skilled positions boast higher voluntary turnover rates, lower levels of engagement, and higher material wages with a performance level typically equal to or worse than their experienced, non-degree-holding colleagues with the same job.[7] Value is found in the individual, not the credential.

Eliminating bias is an introspective and active process in creating a Win-Win workplace. First, by focusing on skills and competencies for a position instead of credentials, you open your talent pool to those with relevant skills but nontraditional experience. Second, using objective, data-driven tools to evaluate candidates' talents, such as skills assessments or performance-based tests, will provide a more accurate picture of each candidate's potential, which helps hiring managers overcome unconscious biases on hiring. Third, employers can train managers to recognize and avoid bias in hiring practices, starting with diversifying the hiring team itself to include people with various backgrounds and perspectives. Lastly, by integrating diversity into workplace culture and values, companies can foster a culture of respect and inclusion. They're poised to set diversity goals, track progress toward those goals, and support members of underrepresented groups with appropriate resources.

SKILLS-BASED TALENT OPTIMIZATION: IDENTIFYING COMPETENCIES, NOT DEGREES

Hiring STARs is a terrific example of skills-based talent optimization because it emphasizes that understanding a worker's roots and providing training based on an assessment of that individual's capabilities fosters competency, regardless of credentials or prior experience. This skills-based approach enables companies to pivot with greater confidence since the workforce has already demonstrated a capacity to retain and execute new skills as required. By hiring STARs, an organization demonstrates its ability to leverage the employee's past experience to serve emerging and temporary organizational needs.

Skills-based talent optimization starts with identifying specific competencies and abilities required for a particular position. Then managers select candidates or promote internally based on demonstrated skills and not just formal qualifications. Leaving behind traditional talent practices that champion degrees and social connections above all else, companies save on hiring and payroll costs by attracting nontraditional candidates that may demand less competitive salaries. Your non-degreed hires may also have a stronger sense of loyalty to your company, especially if they had a history of being rejected only because they didn't have the expected degree.

Instead of searching for a degree, skills-based talent optimization looks at *what skills the job actually requires for good performance.* By identifying required skills, managers avoid poor hiring decisions, reducing employee turnover and training expenses while increasing productivity.

To determine the skills required for a position, conduct a job analysis by gathering information about a job's duties, responsibilities, required skills, and qualifications. Sources for this analysis include interviews with employees, surveys, or observing those employees who are already performing well in the position. From these sources, create a job description that outlines the expectations for the position.

The Win-Win workplace demands that hiring managers consider the large pool of talented and qualified candidates with nontraditional sources of skills as part of the mission to create a more diverse and inclusive workforce. This mission includes debunking the notion that a four-year degree is necessary for job-relevant skills. It means, as previously noted, breaking the myth that low-wage means low-skill. Hiring based on skills and not degrees represents a step toward a more inclusive future that may provide upward economic mobility for those previously excluded from hiring conversations.

ADOPTING SKILLS-BASED TALENT OPTIMIZATION: WHEN YOU WISH UPON THE STARS

Today, technology has the potential to quickly and radically alter an economic sector in a matter of weeks or months. Large language models like ChatGPT are stirring the pot. They offer businesses a tool to automate tasks and boost productivity in areas like content creation and customer service. This could lead to job shifts, potentially impacting high-income analytical or creative roles more than manual labor jobs. However, this disruption also creates opportunities in managing AI tools, ensuring data security, and navigating human-AI collaboration. The key lies in addressing ethical concerns around bias, misinformation, and potential job displacement to ensure this technology benefits the overall economic landscape. This means that malleable skills are more necessary than training tailored to specific jobs or industries. The World Economic Forum estimates that over 1 billion people will need reskilling by 2030.[8] Focusing on skills enables organizations to assign activities to individuals based on their unique capabilities. Broad, amorphous, mandatory training—that assumes all employees are following identical career trajectories with identical career goals—must be left in the past. Focusing on skills develops organizational flexibility and agility. It also empowers employees to build skills that are more easily transferable between companies and industries.

WHAT THE RESEARCH SAYS

My analysis of data from 1,200 companies shows many are moving toward using flexible teams. These teams can change and adapt quickly to meet the fast-changing needs of the business. In fact, a recent Deloitte Global Human Capital Trends survey found 76 percent of C-level executives rated internal talent mobility as "important." Twenty percent of C-suite executives placed internal talent mobility among their organization's three most urgent issues. Yet, only 6 percent of the senior executives surveyed described their organization as "excellent" at enabling internal talent mobility.[9] This indicates a significant gap between the importance placed on internal mobility and the actual effectiveness of enabling it within companies.

Case Study: *Jergens Sets Up Employees for the Future*

Jergens, Inc. has always been a family business. The Cleveland-based company, which specializes in manufacturing workholding equipment, is still owned by its founding family. Jergens employees are part of the family. And like any good family, each member works to improve both their own lives and those of the rest of the family members.[10]

Jack Schron Sr. founded Jergens in 1942, during the height of World War II. To contribute to the country's war effort, his goal was to train workers, just as much as it was to make profits. The company's philosophy was simple: "Do the right thing for our people, our community, and the environment." The war was won and Jergens earned its reputation as a company that enriched its workforce. In essence, Jergens was an early leader in creating a Win-Win workplace, prioritizing employee well-being and fostering continuous learning and development.

When Jack Schron Jr. took over as president and CEO of Jergens in the 1980s, he vowed to uphold his father's commitments in his community, at home and at work. At home, Jack Jr. serves as a Cuyahoga County councilman and a longtime leader in education, workforce development, and community service. At work, he is known as a champion of Northeast Ohio's manufacturing evolution who believes in a "big tent" mentality—that everyone has the potential to be trained to succeed on the manufacturing floor, no matter their background. From this commitment arose Tooling U, a workforce education initiative. Launched by Jergens in 2001 to address a looming skilled-labor shortage, Tooling U offers internships, apprenticeships, and training programs that teach new skills to those with the desire to learn.

After being sold to the Society of Manufacturing Engineers in 2010, Tooling U is now the biggest online manufacturing training platform, serving more than half of companies in the Fortune 500. It has trained more than eight hundred thousand learners in courses from basic blueprints to advanced welding. As Jack Jr. explained, "Education raises the level for everyone who wants to enhance their lives, not only those earning degrees, but those who want to learn a skill." Jergens pays for its employees to attend skills development courses and acquire training. The company strives to offer every individual, regardless of their starting position, an opportunity to move up.

As part of their "big tent" mentality, Jergens actively recruits STARs. The company works with local workforce development organizations like the Cuyahoga East Vocational Education Consortium to train nonemployees as an opportunity to scout and recruit talent. He actively welcomes individuals with disabilities to the manufacturing floor and, unlike many companies, doesn't rule out applicants with prior convictions. According to Jack Jr., the recidivism rate among their employees is zero.

In total, these STARs-based strategies save Jergens approximately $100,000 per trained individual. That figure does not include financial benefits gained through post-training. Those who received training from Jergens are among that company's top performers. Jergens' commitment to employee growth contributes to the company's family atmosphere. Their employees return Jergens' investment in them, working harder and staying longer. Some individuals start working for Jergens in high school and eventually grow into leadership positions.

EQUIPPED FOR THE FUTURE: USING EMERGING TECHNOLOGIES

Emerging technologies can be partners in creating an equitable future of work. Moreover, the value of skills rooted in technology will only increase. In the future, it is easy to imagine that certain technological skills will be a necessary part of every conceivable position—if they are not already. Comfort with emerging technologies is a necessity, especially when it comes to improving business outcomes.

Yet, there also should be *dis*comfort with emerging technologies to some degree. It is not about the uncertainty of the future of technology; it is not a fear that the robots will become sentient and steal our spouses by eclipsing our meager human ability to listen. Rather, the discomfort is that the information surrounding the technology is often concealed. Want to know what factors are used in an algorithm? The answer will frequently be, "It is proprietary." How does it function? "Machine learning." What are the inputs given to the machine to learn? "It's proprietary." When algorithms aim to eliminate bias, there is always the risk that they were programmed, either intentionally or not, to maintain existing biases. Joy Buolamwini, activist and founder of Algorithmic Justice Leagues, puts it perfectly: "The machine is learning a representation of the world that is skewed. And so what you might have thought should be a neutral process is actually reflecting the biases that it has been trained on."[11] It is crucial that we actively subvert the biases ingrained in AI algorithms and ensure that we develop and utilize this technology responsibly.

ARTIFICIAL INTELLIGENCE: OUR FRIEND IN THE FUTURE

AI-powered workforce analytics platforms offer companies an objective and efficient way to identify, develop, and retain the most qualified talent. Research suggests that workforce analytics platforms that use machine learning to identify and develop talent can have a significant impact on organizations. Here are some key findings:

- **Better hiring decisions:** A 2022 McKinsey & Company study found that companies that use data analytics for talent acquisition are more likely to make better hiring decisions and reduce employee turnover.[12] Workforce analytics platforms that use machine learning can help organizations identify the right candidates for the job based on their skills and potential, rather than their credentials alone.

- **Improved talent management:** A 2023 study by Deloitte found that organizations that use predictive analytics for talent management are twice as likely to improve their leadership pipeline, and 2.5 times more likely to improve their talent practices than those that do not.[13] This suggests that workforce analytics platforms that use machine learning can help organizations make better decisions about talent management.

- **More efficient workforce planning:** 2024 Research by Accenture found that workforce analytics platforms can help organizations optimize their workforce planning by identifying skill gaps and providing insights into employee potential. This can help organizations make better decisions about talent deployment and development.[14]

Skills-based talent strategies present organizations with an enormous data challenge. Effective use of AI can assist companies to determine which skills to leverage in the workplace, and how to leverage those skills in both talent analysis and planning. These capabilities can inform better talent management decisions. Taken to its logical conclusion, AI-driven workplace management tools will be able to help companies better understand trends and both current and emerging skills through forecasting and benchmarking.

To make the most of AI, we need a globally standardized way of organizing job-title and skills-required data, otherwise it's hard to effectively match people with the right skills to the right opportunities. For example, a solar energy technician at Company A needs to set up and maintain solar panels that generate electricity, work on rooftops, and connect panels to electrical systems. In contrast, a solar energy technician at Company B needs to install systems that use sunlight to heat water, work with plumbing, and check energy efficiency. Even though both jobs are called "solar energy technician," Company A focuses on solar electricity, while Company B focuses on solar water heating.

With a standardized system for identifying and classifying skills, it would be easier for AI to accurately match candidates to job opportunities, even when job titles are the same but the required skills are different. To aid in this process, companies should seek to have a universal classification system for skills they intend to measure. This system needs to be pliable enough to demonstrate changes in skills over time, new skills you'll need in the future, and those that require growth and improvement.

Case Study: *Arena Analytics: Using Data to Battle Bias*

Arena Analytics CEO Myra Norton told me that her company uses machine learning algorithms to evaluate skills and competencies of job candidates based on objective data, such as employees' work experience, education, and skills assessments.[5] By focusing on skills and competencies rather than personal characteristics, the platform helps to eliminate unconscious bias that may influence traditional hiring processes.

Jill Thomas, chief nursing officer at a multi-site health system in the Pacific Northwest with 20,000 employees, called upon Myra to help manage her hospital staffing issues. After seeing Myra speak at a health conference, Jill became curious about Arena Analytics' ability to remove bias from the hiring process. Jill's staff was stretched thin and grossly overworked. Patient satisfaction declined, as did quality of care. The hospital's traditional hiring criteria created a workplace where every member had similar credentials. Hiring managers focused on experience, pedigree, and behavioral assessments. Jill sought Arena Analytics' help in resetting the "profile" they traditionally used to hire.

Arena Analytics had two aims: (1) increase applicant flow and (2) stabilize the workforce by reducing turnover. Through their partnership with Arena Analytics, Jill's health system was able to identify individuals who were likely to thrive in their organization. Many of these viable candidates would have been beneath consideration under the previous, traditional hiring methods. With Arena Analytics' help, the hospital increased applicant flow by more than 20 percent, making it possible for the health system to fill its open positions and improve the quality of care for the communities it serves.

In addition, by discarding the antiquated "profile" of an ideal candidate, community members who never considered a career in healthcare entered the profession, embarking on a trajectory that enables economic mobility for themselves and their families. Through Arena Analytics' platform, 16 percent of applicants were hired for a job they **_did not_** originally apply for, and applicants submitted 18 percent more applications than through traditional means. These are both measures of the opportunities the new hiring system has created.

The financial impact of this work has been equally significant. The health system filled many positions, including new hires in direct patient care, customer service, the lab, transportation, and others. Turnover dropped by 35 percent, saving the organization more than $20 million annually. More than that, using Arena Analytics' platform enabled fundamental changes to the health system's structure to sustain these benefits in the future.

These advanced, AI-driven tactics spot and stop unconscious bias from influencing hiring decisions. They have proven to be a viable mechanism for reducing the perpetuation of like-seeking-like, where homogenous hiring teams favor homogenous applicants, and homogenous leadership chooses homogenous employees for internal advancement. Wide implementation of this technology has the potential to bolster socioeconomic mobility.

As the job market continues to evolve, the ability to hire for skills will become increasingly important for organizations looking to stay competitive, adapt to changing circumstances, and create a culture where all members of the organization can win.

Process of Change: *Six Steps to Rethinking Credentials*

Prepare

1. **Identify opportunities to center employee voice:**

   - Conduct surveys and interviews to engage current employees and gather insights on the essential skills required for success in their roles.
   - Organize focus groups and facilitate discussions with employees from diverse backgrounds to identify practical skills and attributes necessary for different positions.
   - Use the gathered information to pinpoint gaps in the current hiring process and opportunities for integrating skills-based assessments.
   - Interview employees who excel in their roles and observe day-to-day activities to create detailed job attribute profiles highlighting key skills and behaviors.

Act

2. **Prioritize setting up skills-based hiring strategies:**

   - Focus on required skills and competencies when developing detailed job descriptions rather than traditional qualifications such as degrees or years of experience.
   - Incorporate practical tests and skills assessments into the hiring process to objectively evaluate candidates' abilities.

- Leverage technology by investing in applicant tracking systems and algorithms that match candidates' skills with job requirements, reducing biases in the hiring process.
- Create training programs and educate hiring managers and human resources staff on the importance of skills-based hiring and how to effectively assess candidate skills.

Refine

3. **Engage with employees to develop new approaches to skills-based hiring:**

   - Hold collaborative workshops where employees can contribute ideas for refining the skills-based hiring process.
   - Conduct pilot programs to test new approaches in select departments, incorporating employee feedback to ensure practical application and effectiveness.
   - Encourage employees to share their experiences and suggest improvements based on their unique perspectives and expertise.

4. **Evaluate outcomes and adoption of new approaches:**

   - **Use metrics:** Assess the impact of skills-based hiring by tracking diversity of hires, performance of new employees, and overall job satisfaction.
   - **Collect feedback:** Gather input from hiring managers and new hires to gauge the effectiveness of the new strategies.
   - **Review adoption rates:** Regularly review how widely and effectively the skills-based hiring process is being adopted across the organization.

5. **Adjust new approaches as needed:**

   - **Make necessary adjustments** to improve the skills-based hiring process.

- **Stay updated:** Keep abreast of best practices and emerging trends in skills-based hiring to continuously refine your strategies.
- **Ensure consistency:** Communicate adjustments clearly and implement them consistently across the organization.

Communicate and Learn

6. **Communicate regularly:**

- **Provide regular updates:** Share ongoing progress and outcomes of the skills-based hiring initiatives through newsletters, meetings, and internal communications platforms.
- **Highlight success stories:** Share testimonials from new hires and hiring managers to illustrate the positive impacts of the new approaches.
- **Create a feedback loop:** Encourage continuous feedback and open discussions about the skills-based hiring process to further foster trust.

Implementing a skills-based hiring process may face resistance to change, lack of buy-in from hiring managers, and difficulty in finding suitable assessment tools. To overcome these challenges, organizations should develop a communication plan to ensure that all stakeholders understand the benefits of skills-based hiring and provide ongoing support and training to hiring managers and recruiters to ensure that they can effectively implement the new process. Partnering with external consultants and industry experts can also provide valuable guidance and resources for implementing a successful skills-based hiring process. Thus, numerous strategies exist to position a company to best leverage the significant benefits conferred by skills-based hiring.

By adopting a skills-based hiring process and utilizing skills intelligence platforms, organizations can attract and retain top talent, increase productivity, and create a more diverse and inclusive workplace, reaping the benefits outlined in the Win-Win process of change. By rethinking credentials, companies can tap into a broader pool of talent, build a more inclusive workforce, and ultimately find the best person for the job. This can lead to greater innovation, improved problem-solving, and a more successful business.

While we learned in this chapter that reimagining credentials opens the door to a wider range of qualified candidates, organizations need a strategic approach to cultivate and develop that talent. In Chapter Seven, we'll explore strategies to build a deep talent bench, ensuring you have a pipeline of skilled individuals ready to step into key roles and contribute to your organization's success. Let's turn the page.

CHAPTER SEVEN

DEVELOPING DEEP TALENT BENCHES

We all know the irresistible appeal of something shiny and brand-new. Hiring managers are not immune. Too often, they scout new faces and toss big money at new, untested talent with impressive credentials. But what about the talent already hard at work for the organization? In a Win-Win workplace, internal talent is trained for growth and primed for promotion. The last thing you want is for that internal talent to walk out the door.

Katie's Story: *Too Little, Too Late: Institutional Failure to Recognize Potential*

Katie Sievers, a self-described opportunity expander, was never one to wait on the bench until called into action. With a natural drive to always be looking for the next big problem, she thrived in the fast-paced, mission-driven world of a young education technology startup. She rocketed from customer success to consulting lead and was constantly learning and growing. While the changes in her role were not formal promotions, the company's agile team culture and freedom to propose and execute on new projects kept Katie highly engaged. Every day brought a new challenge, and she eagerly stepped up to the plate. But one nagging question lingered: Where was the path to the next rung of the ladder? The overall strategic direction of the company and, more personally, the question of titles—and perhaps a raise—remained shrouded in ambiguity.

Then the game changed. Acquisition of the young startup she worked for by a global education giant promised a new scale of impact but imposed restrictions on the scope of Katie's role and her visibility into organizational priorities. She was moved under a new manager who she felt didn't understand or value her work— at a time when the department was facing problems that Katie felt she could help solve if given the chance. Two years in, Katie found herself adrift and disappointed by the lack of opportunity to drive change.

"I went from feeling trusted to shape my role to being put into a box with no windows," Katie recalled to me in an interview.[1] "It felt like my colleagues, and I were just data points in a system, with no agency over our work or the broader success of the business."

Meanwhile, the company started rounds of layoffs. Processes started breaking down as people with key skills and knowledge left the organization. It was clear that whoever was making personnel decisions lacked critical information about people's roles and abilities. Katie began looking for opportunities elsewhere.

Here's the rub: Katie wasn't alone. This global giant, with its vast resources, had missed the opportunity to leverage her potential and that of others like her. Katie was part of a talent gap waiting to be bridged. What if, instead of making opaque personnel and layoff decisions, the company had shared its vision and recognized its employees' unique potential to contribute value? What if they'd created a "deep bench" designed with employee success in mind?

THE RISKS OF ZERO-SUM HIRING

According to workers I interviewed, it is not uncommon for employers to offer large bonuses and competitive salaries to attract new talent while simultaneously, and seemingly blindly, leaving internal top talent to languish unfulfilled—or quit. This Zero-Sum strategy tosses money to candidates without proven loyalty or demonstrated potential, and may, in turn, demoralize those already on staff being overlooked for the same position. In a Win-Win workplace, the hiring strategy *starts* by looking internally for assets just waiting to be discovered, instead of buying into the unknown candidates.

Developing deep talent benches, or cultivating a robust pool of skilled and experienced employees across various levels and functions, is crucial for several reasons. Firstly, it ensures continuity and stability within an organization by mitigating the risks associated with turnover and succession gaps. Secondly, a deep talent bench facilitates knowledge transfer and cross-functional collaboration, fostering a culture of learning and innovation. Thirdly, it enhances employee engagement and commitment, as individuals are more likely to invest in their roles and contribute meaningfully when they see opportunities for growth and advancement within the organization.

In this chapter, we'll explore strategies for achieving a deep talent bench. By implementing these approaches, you can increase employee commitment, cultivate depth in your talent pool, and enjoy the bottom-line benefits of longer-tenured employees. Additionally, you'll enhance innovation and efficiency within your organization, leveraging the diverse skills and expertise of your workforce to drive sustainable growth and success.

Katie's Story, Continued: *A Fleeting Win-Win*

With layoffs in the air and bad vibes from her new manager, Katie was ready to cut bait with her employer. But the story didn't end there. On a department-wide call, Katie asked a question that caught the attention of a member of the leadership team and sparked a continued conversation. The leader saw in Katie the ambition and strategic thinking skills that he knew would add value to a different part of the business that was developing a new product and needed a project manager. Although Katie was in a client-facing consulting role and had no prior experience with product management methodologies, she *did* have the industry expertise, solution orientation, and collaboration skills needed to drive this project forward. The leader tapped Katie for a temporary secondment (formally splitting her time between two roles) and gave her the autonomy to figure out how to tackle the task. Finally, Katie had the agency and stretch opportunity she was hungry for. And the leader's intuition was right: the project was a success.

While this leader's instinct was enough to keep Katie with the company for a few extra months, her frustration with the deeper institutional failure to recognize and develop talent was too big a hurdle to overcome. She left for another opportunity shortly after completing the project.

In my research, I interviewed countless workers like Katie. There was Jonathan, a seasoned professional with a weary glint in his eye who described navigating the labyrinth of gatekeepers who guarded access to new opportunities. Karmen, her voice cracking with frustration, yearned for internal mobility, a chance to climb the corporate ladder without hitting an invisible ceiling. And Julie spoke of languishing skills and untapped talent, a poignant reminder of wasted potential and a sobering indictment of organizations that fail to cultivate their own gardens.[2]

These weren't just individual stories; they were brushstrokes painting a stark portrait of Zero-Sum workplaces where talent, the lifeblood of any organization, is an afterthought, and talented employees with untapped potential are left to wither in unfulfilling roles.

THE SILENT DRAIN: WHEN COMPANIES OVERLOOK THE TALENT MINE WITHIN

Imagine a diamond mine, not glittering with cut and polished stones but with human potential. Now imagine it's not buried beneath the earth, but right within your own organization. This is the tragedy of untapped talent; the vast reserves of human potential that companies ignore at their own peril.

The cost? Staggering. It generates a revolving door of employees, with each departure bleeding cash through recruitment, onboarding, and lost productivity. Studies say external hires cost double to onboard and take three to twelve months to reach peak performance, creating a productivity gap of $24,000 per employee. That's a hefty price tag for a shiny new résumé when the *Harvard Business Review* reports internal promotions outperform external hires in all metrics over the duration of the job.[3]

But it's not just the money. It's the morale. The feeling that Katie experienced of being adrift in a sea of ambiguity, her talents unappreciated and her goals unheard or misunderstood. A recent Gallup survey found that only 33 percent of US employees feel engaged at work, with limited development opportunities being a major contributing factor.[4] As we saw in Chapters Two and Three, this disengagement leads to knowledge walking out the door, lost institutional memory, and sputtering innovation. Organizations become rigid, unable or unwilling to adapt to the changing winds of the market.

Why do we cling to the illusion of the perfect external hire when diamonds may be right under our noses? Blame it on the allure of the shiny and new résumé. We chase novelty, overlooking the loyalty, institutional knowledge, and fire already burning within our own ranks. We forget that even the roughest diamond, with the right cut and polish, can become a dazzling gem.

But it doesn't have to be this way. We can create a world where we place more value on individuals' real-world experiences and willingness to learn than on the credentials they earned years ago.

Shaun's Story: *New York–Presbyterian's Hidden Talent Mine*

Shaun Smith was an anomaly. Born in Jamaica, he came to embody the American dream as chief people and culture officer at New York–Presbyterian, one of the nation's healthcare giants. His path, though, was anything but straightforward. A failed pre-med stint opened his eyes to the importance of finding his passion and then led him to human resources. But before that, there were heavy loads to move at the trucking company and, later, deposits to count at the bank—jobs that would shape his approach to talent development.[5]

"I learned a lot unloading trucks," Shaun said to me, his voice weighted with the wisdom earned on his unconventional journey. "Those were skills, competencies I gained. I was a bank teller too, so I can type fast. I was a data entry person. But someone saw something different in me." That "something" was not a pedigree, but potential. And that's the bedrock of Shaun's philosophy. In 2022, faced with a leadership team at New York–Presbyterian that was as homogenous as a Norman Rockwell painting, he could have gone the easy route. He could have stayed with the status quo, prioritizing external hires and job candidates with existing credentials. Instead, he did something audacious. He looked inward.

Here's the thing about hospitals: many are hemorrhaging talent. Nurses flee burnout, doctors chase prestige elsewhere. Globally, turnover rates for nurses hover around 18 percent, and in the United States are even higher—at 28 percent—making hospitals a revolving door of experience and expertise.[6] Shaun saw this not as a problem, but as an opportunity. A diamond mine, right under his nose, buried in underutilized potential.

Enter the apprenticeships, the internships, and the dismantling of the "degree or bust" myth. Under Shaun's leadership, job rotations became passports to new possibilities, shattering the barriers between departments. Stigmas about "lesser" roles were replaced by an ethos of celebrating diverse career paths. Success stories became billboards, each promotion a testament to the power of internal development.[7]

But Shaun didn't stop there. He knew talent wasn't a privilege reserved for the upper echelons. He described to me how he challenged the status quo where menial tasks would be left to early career nurses, arguing that nurturing potential starts at the front line—arguing, essentially, for the Win-Win process of change. He challenged the tradition of assigning night shifts by seniority, arguing for a fairer way to share this responsibility among all staff.

To help upskill his workforce, he worked closely with lower-paid employees to understand their needs and goals, realizing that many were pursuing degrees but not necessarily advancing in their careers within the organization. This led to a shift from a traditional tuition reimbursement model to a more strategic approach where the company would reimburse tuition if there was a link between an employee's studies and career goals and the hospital's internal mobility opportunities. The message to employees changed. Instead of telling workers "We want to help you develop yourself," the message became "We want to grow you so you can grow with us." Plus, a series of "Wednesday Forums" were introduced, at which employees could leave their posts to hear presentations by colleagues from different positions within the organization.

The results? Turnover plummeted by 25 percent. Challenging the assumption that external talent is superior, the company nurtured its internal pipeline resulting in a 50 percent rise in open positions being filled internally, delivering a Win-Win for both employee morale and financial efficiency. And the C-suite, once a monochrome portrait, now reflected the diversity of the community it served.[8]

Shaun's story is a blueprint. It's about looking beyond résumés and titles, about seeing diamonds in the rough and the potential waiting just beneath the surface. It's about dismantling hierarchies, celebrating diverse talents, and investing in the people who are already there, waiting to shine.

Companies like Arena Analytics, which we got to know in Chapter Six, are already taking action, leveraging leading-edge technology to empower organizations to build robust talent pipelines from within. Next, we will explore how Stadler US is tapping their local communities to build a homegrown pipeline of talent.

Case Study: *Stadler US: Leveraging Community Assets, One Apprentice at a Time*

Stadler US Inc., the American branch of the globally recognized Stadler Rail, established its Utah facility in 2016. Recognizing the importance of a skilled workforce, the company faced the challenge of finding qualified personnel in a new location. Stadler US needed to develop a sustainable and economically viable solution to address the shortage of skilled workers in the rail manufacturing industry. Traditional methods of recruitment proved to be insufficient.

Martin Ritter, CEO of Stadler US, championed the implementation of an apprenticeship program based on a successful model Stadler had launched in Switzerland.[9] This program combines classroom learning with on-the-job training, allowing apprentices to gain valuable skills and experience while earning a paycheck. The program offers a range of benefits:

- **Workforce strengthening:** Stadler US can develop its workforce from the ground up through partnerships with local high schools and community colleges, ensuring that the apprentice talent will learn the specific skills required for the company's needs.
- **Educational opportunities:** Apprentices gain valuable skills and certifications through the community college partnership, enhancing their employability.
- **Community impact:** The program provides an alternative path for high school graduates who may not choose a traditional four-year college education.
- **Employee retention:** Apprentices who persist through the program feel invested in by their employer, and, as a result, they feel like they want to stick around.

Stadler's apprenticeship program has demonstrably benefited both the company and its participants. Here's a glimpse of the program's success:

- Globally, Stadler has trained over 1,200 apprentices.
- The program boasts an impressive 85 percent graduation rate.
- Stadler retains 75 percent of its graduates, saving the company on recruitment and training costs.
- The program's success has inspired five other local companies to develop their own apprenticeship programs.[10]

Stadler US's apprentice program serves as a successful model for addressing the skilled workforce shortage. By both developing new talent at the community level and simultaneously offering real-world experience, the program equips young adults with valuable skills and empowers them to pursue rewarding careers. Additionally, the program benefits companies like Stadler by creating a pipeline of qualified workers, fostering a Win-Win situation for all involved. As the program continues to expand and inspire others, it has the potential to revolutionize how Utah, and potentially the United States and the world, approaches workforce development.

STARS ON THE BENCH

Intel is also known for innovative approaches to building its talent bench. Adult learners, including individuals without baccalaureate degrees (here are those "STARs" again!), can benefit from training programs that lead to certificate programs that, in turn, feed into employment opportunities at Intel. In central Ohio, Intel maintains a Semiconductor Education and Research Program that helps individuals transition into high-demand STEM careers.[11] Indeed, Intel's investments in Ohio have been particularly impressive as the company put $20 billion into building two cutting-edge chip factories in Licking County, Ohio—an investment that was accompanied by a $100 million pledge toward educational partnerships.[12]

Intel's programs to build talent benches and leverage STARs are not limited to regions where the company is building new facilities. Across the United States, Intel provides targeted career development support and mentoring to mid-career workers transitioning into careers in information technology. And Intel is a leader in its efforts to retain employees who may experience challenges in the workplace. An internal hotline named "The Warmline" connects employees to case managers who can resolve conflicts within teams and between individual workers and managers, as well as connect workers to sources of support.[13]

In our research of 355 companies, data on Intel confirm the company's superior performance in multiple pillars of the Win-Win workplace. Median worker pay at Intel is far above the national average and the company is among the most generous firms tracked by JUST Capital with respect to employee benefits: employees receive more training every year than at most other firms and Intel offers a range of benefits (pillar four: reimagining employee benefits) such as backup dependent care, childcare support, and employee tuition assistance.[14] Moreover, Intel benefits from a robust employee stock ownership program, with nearly $22 billion in total assets held by almost 79,000 current and former employees (pillar nine: distributing leadership). Saving the best for last: all of these investments and innovations are overseen by a CEO, Patrick Gelsinger, who embodies pillar six: hiring STARs versus prioritizing credentials. Instead of going to college, Gelsinger accepted a scholarship to a vocational school at age sixteen, where he earned his associate's degree. He started at Intel at age eighteen as a technician and never looked back. Now, *that's* a model Win-Win workplace!

WHAT THE RESEARCH SAYS

In our research, we discovered that companies that reimagine their promotion pipelines achieve significant financial outperformance. Analyzing data from 355 Fortune 500 firms revealed that strong internal promotion pipelines significantly reduce short-term attrition rates and boost financial performance, with 38 percent of these companies showing strong asset growth. These results underscore the strategic advantage of cultivating a deep talent bench, fostering employee loyalty, and sustaining organizational competitiveness. Companies should therefore prioritize maintaining a deep talent bench, thereby enhancing both employee retention and financial performance.

Process of Change: *Six Steps to Develop Deep Talent Benches in Your Organization*

Prepare

1. **Identify opportunities to center employee voice:**

   - Conduct talent audits to identify potential leadership candidates across all levels of the organization.
   - Utilize employee surveys, focus groups, and one-on-one interviews to understand their career aspirations, barriers to progression, and support needed for growth. Shaun Smith emphasized the importance of listening to employees and involving them in decision-making processes. He highlighted that employees consistently express a desire for input into decisions that impact them. Smith advocated for creating a comfortable environment where employees feel they can share their talents and perspectives, as this allows the organization to unleash its full potential. He implemented "Wednesday Forums" where employees could learn about different roles and career paths within the organization. This initiative aimed to educate employees about various opportunities and help them navigate their desired career trajectories.

Act

2. **Prioritize setting up deep talent benches inclusion strategies:**

   - Implement mentorship and sponsorship programs that pair diverse talent with senior leaders.
   - Ensure these programs are designed to address specific barriers faced by underrepresented groups and create pathways for their advancement. Shaun addressed diversity gaps at New York–Presbyterian by advocating for

internal mobility programs (e.g., lab technician sponsorship) and measuring diversity metrics across the organization. He emphasized transparency in talent discussions
and a focus on leadership development. Shaun also highlighted CEO support and the need to adapt job descriptions to improve talent acquisition.[15]

Refine

3. **Engage with employees to develop new approaches:**
   - Establish a structured process for identifying and nurtur-
     ing talent for future leadership roles.
   - Formulate clear criteria and metrics for assessing poten-
     tial candidates for deep talent benches. Shaun Smith
     engaged with employees at New York–Presbyterian to
     develop a new approach to tuition assistance programs.
     He worked closely with employees to understand their
     needs and goals, realizing that many were pursuing de-
     grees but not necessarily advancing in their careers within
     the organization. This led to a shift to a more strategic ap-
     proach to tuition reimbursement where the company
     would reimburse tuition for hospital-related roles.

4. **Evaluate outcomes and adoption of new approaches:** Track
   the progress of participants in leadership development programs through performance metrics, promotion rates, and
   feedback. Analyze this data to identify which approaches
   are most effective in preparing employees for leadership
   roles. Shaun Smith evaluated the outcomes of the new tuition assistance approach by tracking metrics like program
   completion rates, internal mobility percentages, and overall
   employee retention. He found that by making the tuition
   program more purposeful and aligned with career goals,
   employees were more motivated to complete their degrees.

The organization also saw a significant increase in internal mobility, with 40 percent of employees achieving career advancement within the first year of the program's implementation.[16]

5. **Adjust new approaches as needed:** Based on feedback and performance data, refine the mentorship, sponsorship, and training programs. This may involve modifying curricula, adjusting pairing criteria, or introducing new support mechanisms to better prepare employees for leadership roles. Based on the initial outcomes, Shaun made adjustments to further refine the tuition assistance program. He centralized the budgeting and administration of certificate programs to have more control over strategic spending. He also started exploring ways to extend educational support to employees' children, recognizing the importance of creating a longer-term talent pipeline and fostering loyalty among the hospital's employees.

Communicate and Learn

6. **Communicate progress in implementing the new approaches:** Regularly update the organization on the progress of the talent development initiatives. Share success stories, key metrics, and insights gained from the implementation of new approaches. Use these communications to reinforce the organization's commitment to building a diverse and inclusive leadership pipeline. Shaun Smith actively communicated the new tuition assistance approach and its successes both internally and externally. He shared learnings with colleagues at other healthcare organizations like Intermountain Healthcare to promote the adoption of similar talent development strategies. Shaun also engaged with the CEO Jobs Council in New York, collaborating with 34

institutions to create 100,000 jobs for New Yorkers through partnerships with educational institutions like the City University of New York.[17]

By systematically applying this process of change, organizations can develop deep talent benches that are intersectional, inclusive, and well prepared to take on future leadership roles.

Imagine a future where every individual's potential is recognized, nurtured, and unleashed. This isn't science fiction; it's the potential of the Win-Win process of change waiting to be realized. The question remains: Will we have the courage to embrace a commitment to developing a deep talent bench and witness the transformation of hidden gems into dazzling STARs, illuminating the future of our organizations? The answer, like hidden talent, is waiting to be discovered.

In this chapter, we learned that there are avenues to widen talent pools by looking within. In Chapter Eight, we'll build on this knowledge to tie our efforts together, as we know that what doesn't get measured doesn't count. In the Win-Win workplace, what doesn't get measured gets cut.

CHAPTER EIGHT

USING HUMAN-CAPITAL REPORTING AS A COMPETITIVE STRATEGY

Transparency wasn't a priority in the old way of doing business. A 2021 research project conducted by JUST Capital analyzed disclosures from the one hundred largest US employers and examined human capital factors such as employment and labor types, job stability, wages, compensation and benefits, workforce diversity, equity and inclusion, occupational health and safety, and training and education.[1] The research found that the disclosure rate was below 20 percent for most of these metrics, since many companies resist reporting metrics unless legally required.

This reluctance to report has changed. Since the US Securities and Exchange Commission adopted new human capital disclosure rules in 2020, public companies have been increasingly focused on these disclosures, with scrutiny from employees, investors, and other stakeholders.[2] Building on a 2021 survey of S&P 500 companies, a recent update by the Gibson Dunn law firm analyzed disclosures by the even larger S&P 100. This update reveals a clear trend: companies are disclosing more. They're expanding the length and breadth of their disclosures, with a slight increase in quantitative data.[3] Here are some of Gibson Dunn's key findings:

- **More is being disclosed:** Seventy-nine companies increased the length of their disclosures, and sixty-six companies covered more topics.
- **Focus on specific areas:** Talent attraction and retention, employee compensation, diversity statistics, workplace safety, and pay equity saw significant increases in disclosure frequency.
- **Rise of DEI:** Discussions around DEI initiatives became more prevalent, with 37 percent of companies disclosing quantitative data on DEI breakdowns. Board oversight of human capital also received increased attention.
- **Consistency in focus:** While the amount of information provided varies, the most common topics discussed remained consistent: talent development, attraction, and retention; COVID-19; and compensation/benefits. Less frequent disclosures included succession planning, employee type breakdowns, quantitative pay gaps, and workforce turnover rates.

This mindset of open disclosure presents two key opportunities. First, transparency is essential for measuring progress. It provides valuable information not only to employees and job seekers making employment decisions but also to shareholders and customers who wish to align their investments with their values. Second, Win-Win companies will lead their peers, enjoying benefits such as increased employee loyalty, heightened investor interest, and enhanced brand awareness that are all associated with companies that proactively share their human capital metrics. In contrast, Zero-Sum companies that delay action will face the challenge of catching up later, as government enforcement and stakeholder interest in human capital metrics grows.

THE WIN-WIN WORKPLACE APPROACH TO HUMAN CAPITAL REPORTING

In a Win-Win workplace, employers use human capital reporting as a key strategy to attract customers and investors while increasing profitability. Simply put, the new world of work will hold companies accountable. Companies that master environmental, social, and governance (ESG) practices can leverage their human capital reporting to gain a competitive edge in the future of work. Publicly demonstrating their commitment to workers' advancement broadcasts their values while increasing transparency, accountability, and profitability. In this chapter, we'll explore how companies leverage measurement as a competitive strategy. This examination will provide insights into implementing measurement strategies within your own company. Doing so will enable you to showcase transparency to both employees and customers, utilize metrics to track the return on investment of new strategies, and construct a compelling case for the adoption of future Win-Win workplace strategies.

Table 1 lists the key data categories and points to include when setting up a system for sharing the most pertinent information about the company's people.

As discussed in Chapter Three, relative to the intersectional inclusion strategies, it is important to disaggregate this data along identity markers to truly understand how people are faring within an organization and to identify areas for improvement. Figure 2 shows examples of metrics that companies can disclose to promote transparency and foster a positive work environment.

Companies should consider prioritizing quantitative measures (e.g., training hours per employee) for each area of human capital while committing to collect qualitative metrics (e.g., how do employees feel about the types of programs of offered) to provide a

Table 1

Human Capital Data Points

Data Points	Description
Wages and compensation	This is information about what employees are paid and the additional financial benefits they receive. This includes salaries, hourly wages, bonuses, stock options, and overtime pay.
Benefits	This point involves details about nonwage benefits that employees receive, such as health insurance, retirement plans, paid time off, parental leave, and life insurance.
Training and development	This is information about opportunities for employees to learn and grow in their jobs, including training programs, certifications, career development plans, mentorship programs, and educational assistance.
Workforce composition	This is information about the makeup of the company's workforce, including diversity metrics, full-time versus part-time, contract versus permanent, seniority levels, and geographic distribution.
Employee wellness	This is information about programs and initiatives to support employees' health and well-being, such as health programs, mental health support, work-life balance, safety programs, and Employee Assistance Programs (EAPs).
Hiring and stability	This is information about how the company hires and retains its employees, including recruitment metrics, turnover rates, tenure, promotion rates, and job satisfaction.

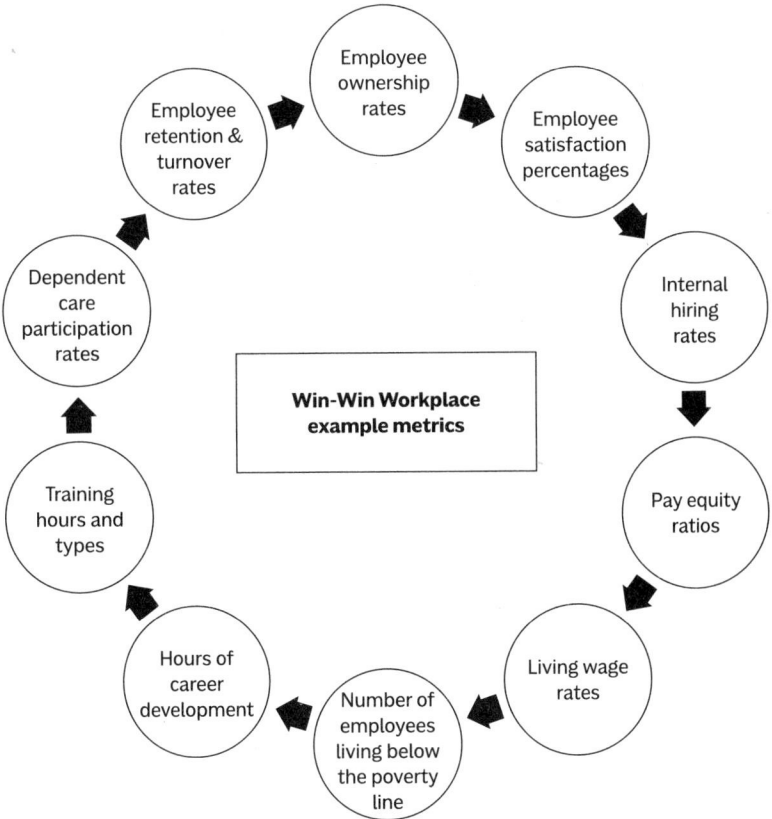

Figure 2. Win-Win Workplace Metrics

business case and comprehensive view of their commitment to a Win-Win workplace.

Here are questions you can ask yourself, your employees, and senior leadership:

Employee-ownership disclosure: Do employees have a say in company decisions?

Hours of career development: How much training do is offered to help employees advance in their careers?

Apprenticeship programs: Are apprenticeship programs offered to develop new talent?

Employee satisfaction: How happy are employees?

Internal hiring rate: How often are individuals promoted from within the company?

Pay equity analysis: Is everyone paid fairly regardless of gender, race and ability?

Living wage disclosure: Do we or can we afford to pay a living wage in the areas we operate?

Retention or turnover rate: How many people stay with the company and how many leave?

Number of employees living in poverty: How many of our employees struggle to afford basic needs?

Dependent care: Do we offer support for employees with equal access to the same dependent caregiving needs?

These questions will help you determine your pathway to becoming a Win-Win workplace. They will also help you benchmark where you are today to prepare the company for using human capital reporting as a competitive strategy. The following case study illustrates how these questions can significantly impact employee wellness and ensure hiring stability.

Natasha's Story: *Transparency Is More Than Just Talk*

Natasha Lamb, cofounder of Arjuna Capital, has built a successful business investing in companies that embrace transparency and equity. Before founding Arjuna Capital, Natasha was a senior executive at a top financial firm. During our interview, she shared with me a personal story that illuminated for her the chain reaction of how a company's human capital practice can impact their retention of talent, which impacts operations, which impacts profitability.[4] When Natasha returned to work from maternity leave after having her first baby, she asked if she could work from home one day per week to spend more time with her child and enjoy a better work-life balance. While the firm granted her request, they said that she would only be paid for a four-day week and her pay would also be reduced to reflect the new schedule. While the firm she worked for was well known for investments aligned with ESG values, it suddenly became clear to Natasha that the firm did not live by these values in its operations. Decision- and policy-making processes were opaque and, in Natasha's opinion, arbitrary and even punitive. There was a major disconnect between what her firm claimed to be and what it actually did.

Instead of taking a pay cut, she left and established her own firm, Arjuna Capital, which invests in companies that provide flexible work schedules while ensuring that employees are paid equitably. Her interest wasn't purely altruistic: her research found that companies with pay gaps for women and people of color performed worse than their peers. Fueled by her belief that these gaps signal how organizations evaluate their employees, she requested that recipients of her investments disclose salary information and rectify pay gaps.[5] After calling for transparency and disclosure, she's seen these companies grow by a factor of three over their competitors while remaining profitable.

Case Study: *The Power of Transparency: Buffer's Radical Openness*

In the competitive world of startups, trust can be a precious commodity. Customers bombarded with options need a reason to believe in a new company, and establishing that trust is often a long and arduous process. Traditional approaches often rely on carefully crafted public image and controlled communication. But Buffer, a social media management software company founded in 2010, dared to be different. It embraced a philosophy of radical openness, a concept that challenged the status quo and transformed its trajectory.

Radical openness for Buffer meant complete transparency about all aspects of its business. This wasn't just about sharing press releases and curated success stories. It meant opening the vault: financial data, employee salaries, internal discussions, and even early product failures were all laid bare. This audacious strategy might seem like a potential recipe for chaos and vulnerability. However, Buffer's experience highlights a powerful truth: transparency, when embraced wholeheartedly, can be a potent tool for building trust and fostering success.

The most immediate benefit of Buffer's openness was the creation of a strong sense of trust with its customers. Instead of seeing carefully crafted marketing messages, potential users saw a company willing to expose its inner workings, warts and all. This authenticity fostered a sense of genuine connection, allowing customers to understand Buffer's values and operations in a way that traditional marketing simply couldn't replicate. This translated directly into user confidence and a higher adoption rate, propelling Buffer's growth.

The benefits, however, transcended its customer base. Buffer's open communication style fostered a sense of collaboration and innovation within its own team. With information flowing freely, everyone felt informed and empowered to contribute. This created a more agile and efficient company—one that was aligned with the Win-Win workplace pillars—where ideas could be quickly tested and refined. Employees felt valued and engaged, which contributed to a positive work environment that played a significant role in Buffer's rapid success.

Within three short years, Buffer reached a staggering 1 million daily customers. While other factors certainly contributed to its success, the impact of its openness is difficult to ignore. It allowed Buffer to attract and retain a loyal user base, build a strong internal culture, and ultimately establish itself as a major player in the social media management landscape. Buffer continues to lead its peers in transparency regarding one of the most taboo areas of the workplace: compensation. For over a decade, Buffer has openly shared its salary information both internally and externally.

Joel Gascoigne, the CEO, emphasizes that compensation is a crucial and sensitive aspect of work, intricately linked to supporting livelihoods and dreams. He highlights that the "choices a company makes around compensation" significantly impact perceptions of fairness and equity. Moreover, he believes that transparency is vital so that team members have "full information about how and why we make the decisions we do around compensation." When asked why they are transparent about salaries, Gascoigne said, "All of this leads to greater trust. We believe that trust is the foundation of great teamwork, and we've learned from over a decade of experience that transparency breeds trust."[6] Buffer's story is a testament to the power of transparency. It demonstrates that trust, built through genuine openness, can be a significant competitive advantage.

However, a crucial caveat remains: Embracing transparency is not a one-size-fits-all solution. Certain industries or companies with sensitive information may require a more nuanced approach, so radical openness may not be right for all organizations. Nevertheless, Buffer's success offers valuable insights for any company seeking to build trust, foster collaboration, and achieve rapid growth. In a world that increasingly demands authenticity, transparency is a key to unlocking a company's full potential.

Ekow's Story: *Opening the Glassdoor for Diversity*

Ekow Sanni-Thomas had worked for thirteen years in corporate finance before leaving the field. In our interview, he described how he'd become tired of the lack of diversity in his workplaces.[7] Their hypocrisy also left him emotionally exhausted. In the wake of the May 2020 death of George Floyd, an unarmed Black man, at the hands of Minneapolis police officers, companies made public pronouncements of their commitment to diversity, anti-racism, and understanding of the needs of Black employees. Ekow looked at these commitments and, while the rhetoric had changed, he didn't notice any appreciable results. He wondered how to hold these Zero-Sum companies accountable in an environment completely lacking in transparency.

Frustrated, he decided to do something. He undertook research to understand their experiences, challenges, and needs. By conducting interviews and surveys with fellow people of color across various industries, he sought to gather and share valuable insights and resources. Ekow told me that, for employees of color in the corporate world, "there's a lot more snakes than there are ladders." He aimed to provide information to fellow people of color, starting with asking workers he encountered: "Would you recommend your company to a person of color?" The questions snowballed from there and yielded several important takeaways:

- People want more results in the areas of diversity and inclusion, not more of what many felt were ineffective DEI programs.
- Companies must close the gap between words and actions.
- Measurement of DEI factors must be positioned as motivators and value-adders in the workplace, not as a stick to enforce compliance.

Ekow's research ultimately inspired him to launch a company called Inside Voices, "the Glassdoor for diversity," a place where organizations can receive honest feedback about the effectiveness of their DEI initiatives. Ekow partnered with Kanarys, a leading firm specializing in navigating sensitive workplace topics and providing data-driven insights to enhance organizational cultures. Through this partnership Ekow gained access to scientifically validated measures and scales that assess key metrics related to inclusion, safety, trust, and experiences of exclusion. Kanarys' expertise in crafting the right questions and benchmarks allowed Ekow to gather comprehensive data on his clients' organizational practices, policies, and employee experiences.

Kanarys' audits of organizational practices and policies, coupled with analysis of people data and employee experiences, gave Ekow a deep understanding of which employee groups are at risk of exclusion and the specific inclusion gaps they experience. This data-driven approach empowered him to define robust strategies and action plans to improve engagement, innovation, and retention in his clients' workforce.

By leveraging Kanarys' solution, Ekow and his Inside Voices team can connect people data with employee insights to obtain a holistic view of the employee experience in his clients' organizations. With this comprehensive understanding, he can make informed decisions, drive meaningful change, and, ultimately, enhance employee engagement, retention, and performance over time.

Through his partnership with Kanarys, Ekow was able to navigate the complexities of DEI measurement with confidence. By leveraging data-driven insights and scientifically validated measures, Ekow and Inside Voices empower organizations to foster more inclusive cultures and drive sustainable business success. Currently, the Inside Voices website boasts over five thousand reviews from major companies, including Google and Deloitte. As they continue to collaborate with Kanarys, they are positioned to make a lasting impact on the DEI landscape within the corporate world.

HOW RADICAL OPENNESS CAN TRANSFORM YOUR BUSINESS

In today's competitive landscape, customers crave authenticity and transparency. A 2023 Edelman Trust Barometer report found that 86 percent of global consumers say trust in a business is a deciding factor in their purchase decisions.[8] Building that trust requires going beyond carefully crafted marketing messages to fostering genuine connections through transparency. It might seem unconventional, but Buffer, a social media management software company, serves as a compelling case study for its effectiveness. The company embraced radical openness and shared everything from its financial data and internal discussions to even early product flops.[9] The results were impressive:

- **Customer trust soared:** Transparency fostered genuine connections with customers. Users felt they understood Buffer's values and mission, leading to a higher adoption rate. Studies by McKinsey suggest that companies with strong transparency practices experience a 20 to 30 percent increase in customer satisfaction.
- **Collaboration took flight:** Open communication within the team empowered employees and fueled innovation. Ideas flowed freely, leading to a more agile and efficient company culture. A study by *Harvard Business Review* found that teams with high psychological safety (created by open communication) are more likely to take risks and achieve breakthrough results.
- **Rapid growth:** Within a few years, Buffer reached a staggering 1 million daily customers. Its willingness to embrace openness arguably played a key role in attracting and retaining a loyal user base.

WHAT THE RESEARCH SAYS

In our research, we found that companies that are open about their employees' information can do better in business. We analyzed data from 355 Fortune 500 companies and found that those using employee data for decision-making saw increases in profits and revenue. However, because not all companies tracked this information, the data available was insufficient to establish a significant overall impact. We also studied how reporting pay differences by gender and race affects financial performance. While being honest about pay equity doesn't directly change financial results, it is still an important way for companies to show accountability. This means that even though pay transparency is crucial, we need additional research to determine how it directly impacts a company's profits and employee turnover.

Process of Change: *Six Steps to Human Capital Reporting as a Competitive Strategy*

Prepare

1. **Identify opportunities to center employee voice:** Start small and build trust internally before going public. For example, implement team huddles where employees share what reporting metrics matter most to them and what metrics they see having the most impact on the business. Additionally, interview other key stakeholders to see what matters to them including investors, customers and members of the communities where you operate. Think back to Ekow and how he created Inside Voices because he was disillusioned when the values of his employer were not operationalized

based on his experience. Proactively seeking to understand your employee sentiment can be used to improve the workplace, or you can take the Zero-Sum workplace approach and read about their experiences on platforms like Inside Voices and Glassdoor, whose anonymity and privacy guidance allows current and former employees to review companies anonymously.[10] This means employers may not have the chance to address specific concerns directly or engage in meaningful dialogue with their employees. This lack of direct communication can hinder employers' ability to understand and improve their workplace culture proactively.

Act

2. **Prioritize using human capital reporting as a competitive strategy:** Identify areas for transparency and define a set of related metrics: Not everything needs to be broadcasted. Proactively identify what information to report, how to source it, and who the key stakeholders are and how it will be measured. Share company goals and progress reports with all employees first, in order to create a sense of ownership and keep everyone informed. Be clear about what information will remain confidential, such as ongoing legal matters or trade secrets. Recall back in Chapter One when the management of C.H.I. Overhead Doors revealed to their employees that the company would be sold and that they would be paid out based on ownership stakes. They asked workers—and trusted them—to keep the information confidential until the public release.

Refine

3. **Engage with employees to develop new approaches to human capital reporting:** What information will be shared will change from time to time depending on government or

public expectations, as when organizations like the US Securities and Exchange Commission issued the 2021 guidance to public companies about new human capital disclosures.[11] Create a framework for how you will communicate updates. As we saw in the Intel case study, they, like many corporations, use their annual reports; others use social media.

4. **Evaluate outcomes and adoption of new approaches:** While what types of information you may share and the channels used to share this information may change based on employee and other stakeholder feedback or to comply with state and federal policies, ensure continuity in the evaluation process. Set up a reporting and evaluation system and schedule to make sure the information about the company's people (like career development, training, and job satisfaction) is accurate and reported correctly. Measure the impact of openness on employee engagement, customer trust, and overall performance. Conduct employee surveys to gauge your team's comfort level with open communication and its perceived impact on their work. Monitor customer sentiment.

5. **Adjust new approaches as needed:** Refine your approach based on your findings. This might involve adjustments to the level of transparency, choice of communication channels, or choice of employee engagement strategies.

Communicate and Learn

6. **Communicate progress in implementing the new approaches, the results of the changes, and learnings from the actions:** Lead by example. The commitment to transparency starts at the top. Leaders must actively model the culture they strive to cultivate. CEOs can host regular "Ask Me Anything" sessions with employees or openly discuss

company challenges in blog posts. Encourage employee participation through suggestion boxes, anonymous Q&A sessions, or open feedback channels. Consider tools such as Slack channels dedicated to open communication. Communicate the progress and results of the changes and share learnings from the actions taken to keep everyone informed and engaged.

By following these steps, your organization can effectively use human capital reporting as a competitive strategy, fostering a culture of openness and engagement.

Remember that building a culture of radical openness is a journey, not a destination. Start gradually, adapt as needed, and keep in mind that the appropriate level of openness may vary with your company's size, industry, and existing culture. By embracing transparency, you can unlock the true potential of your organization and foster a culture of trust, collaboration, and, ultimately, achieve long-term success. Is your company ready to embark on the journey of radical openness? Then turn to Chapter Nine where we explore how distributing leadership via entrepreneurial structures can be a step toward increased transparency and trust while driving innovation and agility in your organization.

CHAPTER NINE

DISTRIBUTING LEADERSHIP

LETTING EVERY WORKER BE AN ENTREPRENEUR

Imagine two employees working side by side. One approaches their work like a renter in an apartment: they complete the tasks outlined in their lease (job description) and move on, doing just what they need to in order to get their security deposit back. The other employee acts like a homeowner: they take initiative, invest in improvements, and care about the overall health of the building (company). Which one do you want on your team?

In this chapter, we'll look at the different ways that employees can be incentivized to care, to stay, and to go the extra mile. We will show how fostering a sense of ownership and entrepreneurship can transform employees into engaged stakeholders. The traditional model of siloed expertise stifles innovation and limits problem-solving, as documented in studies on cross-functional collaboration.[1] To thrive in today's dynamic environment, companies need distributed leadership—that is, spread among adaptable, cross-functional teams with a holistic understanding of the organization's goals. With distributed leadership, employees feel empowered to think and act like owners of the business, rather than just renters (as in the metaphor) or replaceable work machines. Employee-ownership strategies and entrepreneurial structures empower individuals to develop diverse skill sets and take ownership of their work's impact on the bigger picture.

What do I mean by "entrepreneurial structures"? I am talking about the policies, processes, and funding that enable any employee with a promising idea for new business or new efficiencies to pursue that idea. More specifically, entrepreneurial structures include

- time and space for employees to work on their ideas, rather than just their assigned roles;
- dedicated funding and resources to experiment and develop new initiatives;
- coaching and mentoring support to help employees bring their ideas to fruition; and
- a cultural "social license" that allows and encourages employees to step up as leaders with ownership mindsets, without fear of being penalized.

Structures like these are how you implement an employee-ownership strategy—the crucial linchpin of a Win-Win workplace, where employee and company success are mutually reinforcing.

WHY DISTRIBUTED LEADERSHIP WINS THE INNOVATION RACE

Distributed leadership thrives within entrepreneurial structures. In the Win-Win workplace, we define distributed leadership as a leadership style that empowers individuals throughout the organization to take ownership, make decisions, and feel invested in the company's success. It goes beyond simply fulfilling assigned tasks. It encourages people to identify and solve problems that extend beyond their specific roles. A 2015 Oxford study found that companies with distributed leadership, where employees contribute ideas, and collaborate and innovate, are more successful, sustainable and agile.[2] This leadership style emphasizes building relationships, understanding the environment, aligning with the mission, and creating new processes. The Oxford research suggests a gradual shift to distributed leadership by empowering employees, fostering communication, and providing learning opportunities. Senior leaders guide this transition.[3] However, building these "distributed entrepreneurial mindsets" presents its own challenges. Hiring for these qualities requires seeking individuals with initiative and go-getter spirit. Evaluating and developing these capabilities necessitates new approaches, moving beyond traditional metrics to assess an employee's ability to think strategically and contribute beyond their immediate responsibilities.[4]

On the Win-Win workplace journey we have taken together so far, we had to go through a phase of first acknowledging employees' voices as critical data for the health of the organization and critical agents of change. Chapters Two through Eight allowed us to begin imagining workplace structures that are human-centered. Hierarchical structures often reflect a human tendency toward social stratification. Stratification leads to alienation and a drop in meaningful participation, inevitably resulting in a Zero-Sum workplace. Conversely, the Win-Win workplace is about more than just building internally. Internal promotions are meaningless in a structure that only amplifies the voices of those at the very top.

To ensure that workers' voices are centered, organizational structures must be examined and changed to accommodate their voices. Dismantling hierarchies and replacing them with structures that can connect all employees may also lead to additional fostering of talent, and a stronger sense of camaraderie to fortify worker growth. This is the last strategy and the most difficult to implement. It requires truly devoting time to understanding the deficiencies in workflow and the needs of the workforce, empowering the employees as stakeholders, and the leadership as stakeholders, and will most greatly affect the revenue potential of the organization, to, therefore, empower the shareholders as stakeholders. Even more, this strategy is about changing *who* is a stakeholder in the company's outcome—and empowering employees, leadership, and shareholders simultaneously.

DISTRIBUTED LEADERSHIP OFFERS NIMBLE ORGANIZATIONS

In 2021, MIT research about nimble organizations—described as adaptable, innovative, and responsive to changes in their environments—showed that their three leadership styles work together to create a culture of innovation and rapid response.[5] Entrepreneurial leaders at lower levels identify new ideas and opportunities. Enabling leaders in the middle to support these efforts by removing roadblocks and connecting them with resources. Architecting leaders at the top, sets the overall direction, purpose, and values that guide everyone. This combination allows the organization to adapt quickly to changing circumstances and seize new opportunities.

The research on nimble leadership highlights ways in which it can be effective in fostering innovation and agility within organizations:

- **Improved innovation:** Studies haven't directly measured the effectiveness of the three leadership styles in isolation, but the combined approach seems to encourage a culture of experimentation and idea generation. Entrepreneurial leaders identify new opportunities, while enabling leaders support their efforts and architecting leaders ensure these efforts align with the overall strategy.[6]
- **Faster decision-making:** Nimble organizations empower employees at various levels to make decisions, reducing reliance

on lengthy approval processes. This allows for quicker responses to changing market conditions or customer needs.[7]

- **Increased employee engagement:** The focus on empowering employees and fostering a culture of ownership can lead to higher engagement and motivation. Employees feel valued for their contributions and have the autonomy to make a difference.

If you've ever visited the Google homepage and delighted in that day's whimsical iteration of the Google logo, or used Google Maps, or checked Google Street View to find the entrance to that parking garage you booked online—congratulations! You already know the fruits of distributed leadership and entrepreneurial structures. Google Doodles, Street View, and Maps are all the successful innovations of Google employees who had a good idea and were encouraged to step outside their lane to develop it. As Lazlo Bock, the former Google senior vice president of people operations, described in his 2015 book, *Work Rules!*, Google created an environment that empowers employees to develop new business ideas and products, rather than just focusing on their assigned roles.

Such an environment has proven profitable for Google and Google employees. What is proven to work involves a reimagining of the prevailing notion of who has a share in the company's outcome. What is proven to work in Win-Win workplaces is allowing workers to feel part of something larger—something working *for* them while they work *for* it. What is proven to work redefines what it means to be successful, exchanging short-term gains for long-term evolution.

In this spirit, I would like to share two more extensive examples of what it looks like for a company to distribute leadership via entrepreneurial structures and reap benefits—not only the return on investment but also the return on impact on your employees and their ability to work on their ideas, rather than just their assigned roles in your company through self-management, flattening organizational structure, and creating pathways for ownership.

Case Study: *Morning Star: Redefining Organizational Leadership through Self-Management*

Morning Star, founded by Chris Rufer, has revolutionized traditional organizational structures with its self-management strategy rooted in basic distributed leadership principles: empowering employees to take ownership of their roles and decisions. With annual revenues approaching $1 billion, Morning Star boasts a workforce of six hundred permanent employees, supplemented by four thousand seasonal workers during peak harvest seasons. Despite its size, Morning Star's success challenges conventional beliefs about the scalability of self-management strategies. Leaders there actively involve employees in decision-making processes, fostering a culture of collaboration and innovation. In turn, the company has realized improvements in productivity, efficiency, and overall employee satisfaction.

Several key conditions contribute to Morning Star's successful self-management model. First, the company operates on the principles of voluntary interactions and honoring commitments, essential for fostering trust and accountability among colleagues. Additionally, a collective framework of mission statements ensures alignment of individual goals with the organization's overarching mission, promoting clarity and purpose.

Central to Morning Star's self-management structure is the Colleague Letter of Understanding, which outlines personal missions and commitments between colleagues. This document serves as a cornerstone for accountability and performance tracking, enabling colleagues to hold each other responsible for agreed-upon tasks.

Morning Star's conflict resolution process underscores its commitment to employee autonomy and collaboration. By empowering employees to resolve conflicts internally and involving third parties only when necessary, the company fosters a culture of ownership and problem-solving.

The bottom-line benefits of Morning Star's self-management approach include increased productivity, enhanced efficiency, improved employee satisfaction and retention, innovation and adaptability, and cost savings. These benefits contribute to the company's long-term financial sustainability and competitive advantage in the market, in essence serving as the ideal case study for the effectiveness of the Win-Win process of change. In addition to the benefits to employee thriving, there is a clear economic case for this structure:

- **Increased productivity and efficiency:** Morning Star's self-management approach drives higher productivity and enhanced efficiency, as employees take ownership of their work and collaborate effectively.
- **Improved employee satisfaction and retention:** Empowering employees through self-management fosters a sense of ownership and autonomy, leading to higher job satisfaction and lower turnover rates.
- **Innovation and adaptability:** By involving employees in decision-making and fostering a culture of collaboration, Morning Star promotes innovation and adaptability, enabling the company to respond swiftly to market changes and challenges.
- **Cost savings and financial sustainability:** The efficiencies gained through self-management contribute to cost savings and long-term financial sustainability, enhancing Morning Star's competitive position in the market.

Morning Star's self-management approach offers valuable insights into the future of organizational leadership. By prioritizing employee autonomy, collaboration, and trust, the company has redefined traditional management paradigms, paving the way for a more agile, innovative, and sustainable future. From this model, we can derive the following recommendations for other companies:

1. Maintaining effective communication and coordination in a self-managed environment can present challenges. Morning Star therefore continually refines communication processes to ensure alignment and collaboration across teams.

2. Equipping employees with the skills and mindset needed for self-management requires ongoing training and development initiatives.

3. Investing in leadership development programs supports managers in fostering a self-managed culture.

4. Implement training and development initiatives to equip employees with the skills and mindset needed for self-management.

Kerry's Story: *Pathways to Becoming an Employee Owner*

Kerry Siggins told me she strived to be an "A-Team" player when I interviewed her in 2023.[8] She moved from Colorado to Texas after college and never planned to look back. When it came time to enter the workforce, Kerry molded herself into the vision of what people wanted to hire: she was smart, ambitious, and desperate to prove herself. But despite her diligent work ethic and determination, Kerry faced numerous challenges in toxic, Zero-Sum work environments characterized by cutthroat competition and minimal support. She quickly realized that her success hinged not only on her own competence and dedication, but on projecting the right image and fitting into the company's "work hard, play hard" culture.

Employees were encouraged to socialize with clients to close deals and were given deep expense accounts to pay for that socializing. A "no excuses" culture demanded that employees meet revenue targets at any cost; failure meant you would be on the chopping block. Beyond the cutthroat environment, there was another huge obstacle to most employees' success: an obscene lack of training. Without training and guidance, Kerry was left feeling adrift and unfulfilled. "I didn't know what I was doing. And, from a cultural perspective, everybody was just there in the office doing their jobs and we didn't have team camaraderie," Kerry told me. She struggled personally—with burnout and drug abuse. Despite achieving success in some of her roles, Kerry's disconnect from the work that claimed such a huge chunk of her life ultimately culminated in a downward spiral and a life-threatening overdose.

Trapped in a cycle primed to keep her from personal and professional satisfaction, Kerry knew that she needed a change. Unsure of her direction but knowing she wanted more out of her work—more out of her *life*—she returned to her Colorado hometown for a fresh start. Then something unexpected happened. Kerry saw a posting for a general manager position at StoneAge, a local, privately owned company in the water-blasting industry. She paused. She had no experience in that area, and she'd never attempted anything like that position. But the idea of working for a small business close to home appealed to her, harkening back to her days as an ambitious twelve-year-old stocking her grand-father's sporting-goods store.

Cofounders John Wolgamott and Jerry Zink launched StoneAge in 1979 after developing a new self-rotary waterjet nozzle in their garage. The founders' passion for research and development bred a culture of product innovation and entrepreneurship, where the commitment to designing new equipment improved water-blasting technology. From the very first minutes of their interview with Kerry, John and Jerry saw her potential. She was not the traditional candidate, and they liked that. More than her background, it was her energy, authenticity, and curiosity that resonated with them— because, to John and Jerry, their people were the most important part of the business.

They told her about their investment in their employees—a promise that when the company benefits, the employees benefit. The pair explained that innovations in water-blasting were only matched by their groundbreaking approach to valuing their employees. Kerry's job offer included a stake in the company: a 25 percent discount on the stock price and an early dividend for participating employees to help them manage the tax burden.

StoneAge's entrepreneurial culture and the employee-ownership mindset "was everything I was looking for," Kerry recalled. "They took a huge risk on me, but I wanted to take all of those experiences [in Texas] and figure out how to lead in a way that people felt supported, felt like they belonged, but also had autonomy to do their jobs." Centering employee voices came naturally. "That was really easy because I had no idea what I was doing and so I had to ask about everything. The secret to my success those first couple of years was that I just asked people, 'What do you think we should do?'"

Today she is the CEO. In 2007, the year Kerry joined StoneAge, the company made $8 million in sales. Today, their sales exceed $75 million annually. Kerry herself is also a multimillionaire, along with 66 percent of the company's employees in the stock owner-ship program. StoneAge's investment in its employees manifests in its economic success. They are one of a small but rapidly increasing number of companies that have created impressive and durable growth, in part through an Employee Stock Option

Plan (ESOP). StoneAge's outcomes data show that making employees shareholders encourages them to feel more valued, maintains employee longevity, and therefore allows them to make decisions in the best interests of the company. Because, in the end, they all *share* in the success. By rethinking employees as partners, organizations get employees who work harder, stay longer, and actively participate in their organization. Burnout decreases; productivity increases. It turns out that happiness is a prerequisite for success, not a by-product of it, and this sequence holds true when the metric for success is increased profit.

FINDING MEANING AND PURPOSE AT WORK

Kerry's story—her lack of purpose, alienation from her work and workplace, and abject unhappiness fueling suboptimal performance—is familiar to many workers. In 2020, amid the COVID-19 pandemic, many workers were forced to reevaluate their relationship with their jobs, seeking greater purpose and alignment with their work. Prior to the pandemic, a Deloitte study found that nearly 70 percent of professionals felt their employers were not doing enough to prevent or alleviate burnout.[9] In 2024 research from the Society of Human Resources, 44 percent of employees reported feeling burned out from work.[10] The report found that the burnout significantly impacts businesses, as affected workers are nearly three times more likely to be job hunting. However, fostering a strong sense of belonging at work can help; employees with a strong sense of belonging are 2.5 times less likely to experience burnout. This underscores the importance of a positive workplace culture in promoting employee well-being and retention.

As a result, employees' expectations for their employers are on the rise. The days of Boomers bragging, "I used to walk ten miles in the snow to get to school" are waning, with the Gen X generation in senior work positions at the same time they are taking care of both their kids and their parents. Millennials are stifled by their lack of economic mobility as the economy keeps buckling beneath them. And Gen Z? Well, they do not care what you think. They just want to follow their bliss. This evolving landscape has led some in these younger generational cohorts to turn to resources such as *How to Do Nothing*, *The Good Enough Job*, and *Four Thousand Weeks* to seek guidance on how to lead lives that don't solely revolve around work.[11] The popularity of this type of book is on the rise, reflecting a broader desire for a more balanced approach to life. It's a call to shift from the employee mindset to the ownership mindset. It's essential for managers to recognize that their talent pool is undergoing a profound reevaluation of work. Now is the time to engage them in a new approach to maintain future competitiveness.

WHAT THE RESEARCH SAYS

In my research, we explored distributed leadership via entrepreneurial structures and their effects on the workplace by analyzing data from 355 Fortune 500 firms. Our findings indicate that these structures significantly influence both workplace dynamics and overall performance, with 37 percent of companies demonstrating strong revenue growth and 40 percent showing strong performance in assets.

We also examined the effects of fostering and investing in internal leadership development, matching employee charitable donations, and offering an ESOP on firm performance. In the United States, employee ownership presents a compelling case for both businesses and workers. Our research showed that Fortune 500 companies that engage in these practices tend to achieve robust, positive financial outcomes, including increased revenue, valuation, assets, and profitability. These results highlight the benefits of inclusive and supportive corporate structures, which utilize financial capital to catalyze change and enhance employees' sense of ownership over company outcomes. Looking nationally, there are 6,533 ESOPs in the United States, holding total assets of over $2.1 trillion. The number of unique companies with an ESOP is approximately 6,322 (5,866 private companies) and (456 publicly traded companies), with 14.7 million participants at companies at all sizes.[12] Studies show a small but positive correlation between employee ownership and firm performance, including increased productivity, sales growth, and profitability.[13] There's also evidence that firms with more employee participation see a stronger performance boost. This might be due to a more invested and engaged workforce.[14]

For employees, ownership translates to greater financial security. Employee owners tend to have higher wages, retirement savings, and job tenure compared to their non-owning counterparts.[15] Additionally, they report feeling more secure in their jobs and satisfied with their compensation and benefits.[16] Employee-owned businesses are also more likely to invest in training and development for their workers.[17] Overall, employee ownership in the United States appears to be a Win-Win situation, leading to a stronger and more stable business environment while improving the financial well-being and job satisfaction of employees.

Research in the United Kingdom shows that employee-owned businesses (EOBs) are often more profitable and offer more benefits to employees, communities, and the environment compared to companies that aren't employee-owned.[18] With a sample that included over 9 percent of the United Kingdom's 1,650+ EOBs, the researchers found that these businesses were 8–12 percent more productive per employee

(Continued)

> **WHAT THE RESEARCH SAYS** (Continued)
>
> than non-EOBs. This boost in productivity comes with several benefits:
> - Higher bonuses and dividends for employees
> - Fewer layoffs over the past three years
> - Higher minimum wages by about £2,900 annually. Compared to non-EOBs, EOBs are twice as likely to have fair wage–related accreditations in place and more likely to offer supported access to healthcare and mental health resources and to invest in employee training, resulting in employee motivation and job satisfaction.
>
> The Employee Ownership Association, which sponsored the research, concluded that by investing more in their employees, these businesses are driving growth that supports a stronger and fairer economy, more resilient communities, and a healthier planet.

To ensure that workers' voices are centered, organizational structures must be examined and changed to accommodate them. Dismantling hierarchies and replacing them with structures that can connect all employees may also lead to additional fostering of talent, and a stronger sense of camaraderie to fortify worker growth. To understand the solution, we must focus on the following process of change.

Process of Change: *Six Steps to Implementing Distributed Leadership via Entrepreneurial Structures*

Prepare

1. **Identify opportunities to center employee voice:** Conduct surveys, focus groups, and feedback sessions to gather input

from employees on decision-making processes and areas where their voices can be amplified. For example, implement a suggestion box system, both physical and digital, where employees can submit ideas and feedback anonymously if desired. Kerry Siggins shared with me her approach to centering employee voices at StoneAge by actively seeking their opinions and ideas on how to solve problems and improve the company.[19] She empowers employees by giving them autonomy to do their jobs and implement their ideas, acting as a catalyst to help bring these ideas to fruition. Kerry fosters a culture of curiosity by asking many questions to learn from employees and creates an environment where they feel supported and like they belong.

Act

2. **Prioritize setting up distributed leadership via entrepreneurial structures:** Establish pilot projects that allow teams to manage themselves and make key decisions independently. This takes us back to Morning Star's self-management strategy rooted in distributed leadership principles.

   - **Create cross-functional teams:** Provide them with the autonomy to handle specific projects or initiatives, along with the necessary resources and support.
   - **Clearly define goals and expectations:** Allow teams the freedom to determine their approach to achieving these objectives.
   - **Empower teams by restructuring them:** Enable them to be more self-managed by giving team members the authority to make decisions, solve problems, and hold each other accountable.
   - **Invest in training and development programs:** Equip employees with the skills needed to thrive in a self-managed environment.

Refine

3. **Engage with employees to develop new approaches to distributed leadership via entrepreneurial structures:** To empower distributed leadership, companies can co-create strategies with employees through workshops and brainstorming sessions, ensuring diverse perspectives are heard (e.g., design thinking workshops). Additionally, reviewing and potentially reducing management layers can create a more accessible leadership structure. Encouraging senior leader interaction with frontline employees and clear communication throughout the transition are crucial considerations.

   • **Evaluate outcomes and adoption of new approaches:** Measure the effectiveness of the new leadership structures by tracking key performance indicators (KPIs) such as employee engagement, productivity, and innovation. Use employee surveys, performance metrics, and feedback loops to assess the impact of distributed leadership on team performance and satisfaction. Regularly review the data collected and adjust strategies based on insights gained.

   • **Adjust new approaches as needed:** Continuously refine and improve the distributed leadership model based on ongoing feedback and performance results. Implement a quarterly review process where teams can provide feedback on the leadership structure and suggest improvements. Be open to making changes and iterating on the leadership model to better suit the needs of the organization and its employees.

Communicate and Learn

4. **Communicate progress in implementing the new approaches:** Regularly update the organization on the progress and outcomes of the distributed leadership initiatives. Use

internal newsletters, town hall meetings, and company-wide emails to share successes, challenges, and lessons learned. Kerry shared that she errs on the side of full transparency in all areas of the business and advises that this transparency builds trust.

By systematically applying this process of change, organizations can effectively implement distributed leadership and entrepreneurial structures, fostering a culture of openness, innovation, and shared ownership.

The traditional pyramid of leadership is crumbling. Hierarchical structures, once seen as the bedrock of organizational success, are giving way to a more collaborative and empowering approach: distributed leadership within the Win-Win workplace. This shift isn't merely about making employees feel good; it's a strategic move with a demonstrably positive impact on the bottom line. Flatter organizations, where employees feel like valued stakeholders, not just cogs in a machine, foster a culture of innovation and propel companies forward in a rapidly changing marketplace.

The path to a thriving future lies in dismantling the hierarchical walls of the Zero-Sum workplace, empowering employees at every level, and sharing in the proceeds of business success. By embracing distributed leadership, companies can unlock a wellspring of creativity, improve decision-making, and cultivate a workforce that is both engaged and adaptable. The resources provided here serve as a road map for those seeking to embark on this transformative journey. Remember, the future belongs to organizations that dare to challenge the status quo and empower their greatest asset: their people.

CHAPTER TEN

HOW TO MEASURE IMPACT AND ROI IN THE WIN-WIN WORKPLACE

We live in a results-driven world, and being able to demonstrate the impact and return on investment (ROI) of the Win-Win workplace is crucial. This is true for businesses seeking profit, nonprofits aiming for social good, and everything in between. But how do we measure success without getting bogged down in numbers and losing sight of our core purpose?

The purpose of this chapter is to guide you on evaluating the effectiveness of the strategies outlined in the book. The chapter explores strategies to effectively assess impact and ROI while staying true to the value of treating human capital as the organization's most important resource.

UNDERSTANDING THE WIN-WIN WORKPLACE ROI

ROI is a familiar concept in business, but its application extends beyond just profits. In the context of creating a thriving workplace, ROI measures the value generated from investments made in employee well-being, engagement, and overall work environment. This value can be financial, social, or organizational, all contributing to a more successful and sustainable company. A Win-Win workplace goes beyond ping pong tables and nap pods. It fosters a culture that drives success.

Therefore, ROI in the workplace encompasses three dimensions:

- **Financial ROI:** This includes quantifiable benefits like increased productivity, reduced absenteeism, and improved employee retention. These translate to cost savings and revenue growth.
- **Social ROI:** This measures the positive impact on employee well-being, satisfaction, and morale. A happier workforce fosters better collaboration, innovation, and customer service.
- **Organizational ROI:** This focuses on the overall health and efficiency of the organization. It considers factors like improved talent acquisition, stronger employer brand, and a more adaptable company culture.

TANGIBLE AND INTANGIBLE RETURNS: A BALANCED VIEW

While financial ROI holds undeniable importance, the traditional Zero-Sum approach to workplace ROI focuses *solely* on the bottom line and can paint an incomplete picture. It's the intangible returns, like employee well-being and a strong company culture, that are central to a Win-Win workplace for long-term success.

A Win-Win workplace fosters loyalty, attracts top talent, and fuels innovation. It's these intangible elements that often lead to the tangible benefits like increased productivity and revenue growth.

By incorporating both tangible and intangible returns, organizations can make informed decisions about workplace investments, creating a holistic approach to success.

Case Study: *Blackstone's ROI Framework for Career Pathways*

One of the key figures advancing this vision is Marcus Felder, principal and head of Career Pathways in Portfolio Operations at Blackstone. As a regular panelist at business conferences, Marcus shares Blackstone's strategies to improve the talent networks of companies it invests in. At the 2023 Blackstone Career Pathways Summit, Marcus was in conversation with Elyse Rosenblum, founder and managing partner of the talent consulting firm Grads of Life, in a fireside chat. She took an unexpected approach to the conversation with Marcus, pressing him on how Blackstone measures the ROI of the human capital processes and Career Pathways recommendations that are implemented by Blackstone's portfolio companies. He shared with me in our July 2024 interview that the question intrigued him.[1] Blackstone prides itself on adding value to portfolio companies by sharing ways to improve operations, and one area of constant interest was human capital. But how could they measure the ROI these companies were making in their people and on their Career Pathways program?

"It all began with a simple yet profound insight," Marcus reflected, his voice resonating with conviction and humility when I interviewed him in 2024. "We had these incredible companies in our portfolio, each brimming with potential. But to unlock that potential, we wanted to add value with a new approach—one that integrated human capital strategies directly into the portfolio's business objectives." In his role leading the Career Pathways program, Marcus saw an opportunity to reshape how portfolio companies could measure the impacts of their investments in their greatest asset: their people.

Developing a Strategic Framework

Off-stage, Marcus shared with me in an interview his experience seeing how the availability of career pathways for a company's employees was directly tied to the company's bottom-line success—a profitable link that was honed through his years of people-centered work in the nonprofit, consulting, and corporate leadership sectors. All of it fed his vision of crafting a robust ROI framework specifically tailored for human capital. "The goal was clear: to align human capital initiatives with measurable business outcomes," he explained, his eyes lighting up with the passion of someone who had found his calling.

Marcus said that, initially, he knew he would need to get key stakeholders across Blackstone on board with the project. His first order of business was to partner with his vice president, Oliva Hewitt, vice president of the Career Pathways team, who would eventually lead the development of the measurement tool. He went on a listening tour to enlist stakeholders for their feedback and advice. He also spoke to the management of portfolio companies to better understand the value they might find in an ROI measurement tool. He relied on support from the broader Talent & Organizational Performance team in Portfolio Operations at Blackstone as well as asset managers and deal teams. He also leveraged external expertise from organizations like Grads of Life, Elyse Rosenblum's nonprofit talent strategy consultancy that works with leading employers to create skills-first talent strategies.

Key Steps to Implementation

When the Career Pathways team embarked on their mission to implement an ROI framework for Blackstone's portfolio companies, they knew that a thorough and strategic approach was essential. The key steps they took are summarized in the following section.

Process of Change: *Measure Impact and ROI in the Win-Win Workplace*

Prepare

1. **Understand existing methodologies:** The team began by delving deep into understanding the existing methodologies and insights from Grads of Life around skills-based hiring. This initial step provided them with a solid foundation and a clear perspective on the landscape of skills-based hiring and engagement strategies.

Act

2. **Collaboration and analysis:** Marcus then convened his internal team to analyze the data and insights they had gathered. He encouraged his team to think broadly about inclusive practices, emphasizing the importance of a skills-based approach. "We needed to break out of traditional molds and consider how different perspectives and skills can drive business success," Marcus reflected. This collaborative effort led to the identification of key areas where inclusive practices could be integrated effectively into their human capital processes.

3. **Metrics development:** With a robust framework in mind, Marcus worked closely with internal and external partners, including the four portfolio companies that agreed to pilot an ROI approach to develop specific metrics that would allow them to measure the impact of their inclusion efforts. "It was crucial to create a system where we could see tangible results and correlations between our inclusive practices and business outcomes," he noted.

Refine

4. **Ensuring adaptability:** Marcus focused on ensuring that the framework was versatile enough to be applicable across various industries, company sizes, and regions. He understood that a one-size-fits-all approach would not work. "We needed a framework that could be tailored to fit the unique needs of each company while maintaining core principles of inclusion and skills-based hiring," he explained.

5. **Pilot programs and refinement:** To validate the effectiveness of the framework, Marcus initiated pilot programs with a select group of companies. These pilot tests were crucial for gathering real-world data and feedback. "Testing our ideas in real business environments helped us refine our approach and address any challenges that arose," Marcus said. The results from their pilots were promising. Marcus shared, "We developed the tool to help see the benefits of inclusive practice adoption, such as improved retention rates and internal mobility cost impacts." He also highlighted that although it's still early days, they are already observing that usage of the tool helps to reduce hiring costs while more accurately calculating turnover costs for the pilot companies. The insights gained from these pilots were invaluable in fine-tuning the measurement framework.

Communicate and Learn

6. **Continuous improvement:** Continuous improvement was a key component of Marcus's strategy. He maintained an ongoing dialogue with portfolio companies and partners, using their feedback to further refine the framework. "It was a dynamic process of learning and adaptation," Marcus emphasized. Based on the pilot programs, Marcus, Olivia, and their colleagues at Blackstone made refinements in the following areas:

- **Cost of hire assumptions:** Marcus explained, "We realized that companies needed a broader approach for calculating the cost of hiring. Initially, we assumed the cost should be broken down by job category, but it ended up being one flat recruiting fee. The cost of hiring includes things like advertising and the costs of the HR recruiter's time."

- **Exempt versus nonexempt employees:** For companies with large frontline workforces, they needed to separate the analysis into salaried (exempt) and waged (nonexempt) employee categories to better understand retention and mobility.

- **Voluntary versus regrettable turnover:** After calculating the initial cost impact with voluntary turnover, they asked companies to compare it with regrettable turnover. If the difference was significant, it was worthwhile to rerun the analysis, focusing on regrettable turnover.

This iterative approach based on continuous improvement ensures that the framework remains relevant and effective in diverse business contexts.

A LASTING IMPACT

Ultimately, the Blackstone Career Pathways team created a repeatable and sustainable model that companies could use to measure and enhance their inclusion efforts. This model provided a clear road map for organizations to follow, making it easier for them to implement and benefit from inclusive practices. "Our goal was to create a lasting impact by empowering companies to leverage their human capital in ways that drive both inclusion and profitability," Marcus concluded.

Through these strategic steps, the Career Pathways team not only implemented a ROI framework but also set a new standard for how companies can effectively invest in and measure human capital practices as part of their overall business strategy. We saw in Chapter Seven that developing a deep talent bench is a proven way to improve business outcomes. Showing businesses how to measure the investment in human capital as championed by Blackstone's Career Pathways program empowers portfolio companies in the following areas:

- **Attracting and retaining top talent:** By focusing on skills development and creating inclusive hiring practices, companies can attract a wider pool of qualified candidates, leading to a more diverse and innovative workforce.
- **Boosting employee engagement:** When employees feel valued and have opportunities for growth, they are more likely to be engaged and productive, and more loyal to the organization.
- **Improving business performance:** Studies have shown that companies with diverse and inclusive workforces outperform their less diverse counterparts. By measuring the impact of their human capital investments, companies can make a strong business case for inclusion.

Marcus Felder's work has had a ripple effect, not only within Blackstone's portfolio companies but also across the business world. His innovative approach to human capital measurement is helping to make the case for a sustainable Win-Win workplace for all.

IDENTIFYING KEY METRICS: MEASURING PROGRESS ON THE PATH TO A WIN-WIN WORKPLACE

The nine pillars outlined in this book collectively aim to create a Win-Win workplace where employees thrive and, as a result, businesses see a lift in their operations. But how can we track progress and measure the impact of these initiatives? This section focuses on establishing measurable indicators for each strategy, allowing you to gauge effectiveness and adjust as needed.

Pillar One: Centering Employee Voices: Measure employee engagement through surveys, pulse checks, and participation in feedback mechanisms. Most critically, measure the implementation rate of employee-generated ideas and share the outcomes widely. Leverage technology like machine learning and generative AI to gather data and synthesize and share insights more quickly. See the "Global People Leaders" case study in Chapter Five for an example.

Pillar Two: Cultivating Mutualistic Working Relationships: Assess internal collaboration, trust, and conflict-resolution effectiveness through (1) conducting employee engagement surveys and (2) analyzing data from social-media social networks, observational methods, communication-tool analytics, participation in peer recognition programs, and assessments of psychological safety.

Pillar Three: Implementing Intersectional Inclusion Strategies: Identify and monitor intersectional identity markers and demographics across the organization and track progress toward established inclusion goals. Measure employee perceptions of fairness and belonging through surveys.

Pillar Four: Reimagining Employee Benefits: Analyze employee satisfaction with benefits packages and measure utilization rates of various wellness programs. Track percentage changes in benefits that have been newly offered based on employee feedback. Finally, track absenteeism reasons and rates to assess the impact of benefits on employee well-being.

Pillar Five: Activating Frontline Leaders: Track leadership engagement scores, training completion rates, improvements in employee satisfaction, changes in performance metrics, retention rates, 360-degree feedback, and the success rates of your frontline managers' initiatives and people they lead.

Pillar Six: Hiring STARs versus Prioritizing Credentials: Measure the success rate of skills-based hiring initiatives compared to traditional credential-focused approaches and the number of employees impacted. Measure and disaggregate promotion rates by degree attainment.

Pillar Seven: Developing Deep Talent Benches: Track the effectiveness of internal training and development programs by measuring skill acquisition and employee performance improvement.

Pillar Eight: Using Human-Capital Reporting as a Competitive Strategy: Regularly monitor employee sentiment toward communication about company performance, goals, and challenges.

Pillar Nine: Distributing Leadership via Entrepreneurial Structures: Track indicators such as the number of employee-led initiatives, the percentage of employees participating in decision-making processes, improvements in innovation and project outcomes, employee satisfaction with autonomy and leadership opportunities, and changes in overall team performance and productivity.

It's crucial to ensure the chosen metrics directly connect to the objectives of each strategy and ultimately contribute to broader organizational goals. For example, tracking employee participation in suggestion boxes (as discussed in Chapter One) measures the effectiveness of efforts to center employee voices, which ultimately contributes to a more innovative and engaged workforce.

EXPLORING COMMON WIN-WIN METRICS

While specific metrics will vary depending on your unique strategies and goals, the following common measures can be applied across different initiatives:

- **Employee engagement:** Surveys and focus groups that gauge employee motivation, satisfaction, and commitment to the organization.

- **Productivity:** Measures of output per employee or team, taking into account factors like quality and efficiency.
- **Retention rates:** The percentage of employees who stay with the company over a specific period.
- **Cost savings:** Quantifiable financial benefits resulting from implementing new workplace strategies, such as reduced turnover costs.
- **Customer satisfaction:** Metrics that track customer experience and satisfaction, often linked to employee engagement and service quality.

By establishing measurable indicators and aligning them with your goals, you can effectively track progress and make data-driven decisions to create a thriving workplace that benefits both your employees and your organization.

Process of Change: *Six Steps for Creating an ROI Approach to Your Win-Win Workplace*

Prepare

1. **Select Strategy and Objectives**

   - **Clearly define the "Why" for the Win-Win workplace pillar you have selected:** What are you trying to achieve with this strategy? Is it increasing sales, improving customer satisfaction, or something else?

2. **Identify Costs and Investments**

   - **List all costs associated with the strategy:** This includes one-time costs (e.g., software licenses) and ongoing costs (e.g., employee time, marketing spend). You can find examples of associated costs at thewinwinworkplace.com.

- **Factor out any sunk costs:** These are past expenses that cannot be recovered and shouldn't be included in ROI calculations.

Act

3. **Define Measurable Outcomes**

   - **Identify Key Performance Indicators (KPIs):** Choose measurable indicators that directly align with your objectives. These will help track progress and assess success. For example, if your objective is to increase sales, a relevant KPI could be "monthly revenue growth." Additional examples are available at thewinwinworkplace.com.

   - **Set baseline measurements:** Establish a starting point for each KPI before implementing the selected Win-Win workplace strategy. This helps isolate the impact of the strategy.

4. **Project ROI**

   - **Estimate the future impact of the selected Win-Win workplace strategy on your KPIs:** Use historical data, industry benchmarks, or market research to project how much improvement you can expect.

   - **Calculate potential benefits:** Translate the improvement in KPIs into financial terms. This could be increased revenue, cost savings, or improved customer lifetime value.

   - **Calculate ROI:** Figure 3 illustrates how to calculate ROI for your strategy.

Refine

5. **Track, Analyze, and Refine**

   - **Continuously monitor your KPIs:** Track progress throughout the implementation of the strategy.

Step-by-Step Breakdown:

1. **Identify the Benefits and Costs:**

   - Benefits: The gains or returns from the investment.

   - Costs: The total amount invested.

2. **Apply the ROI Formula:**

$$ROI = \left(\frac{Benefits - Costs}{Costs} \right) \times 100\%$$

3. **Calculate:**

   - Subtract the Costs from the Benefits.

   - Divide the result by the Costs.

   - Multiply by 100 to get the percentage.

Figure 3. Calculating ROI

- **Analyze results:** Compare actual results with your projections. Identify any deviations and understand the reasons behind them.
- **Refine your strategy:** Based on your analysis, adjust the strategy to improve ROI.

Communicate and Learn

6. Create the Connection

- **Foster trust through transparency:** Proactively communicate the ROI expectations and timeline to stakeholders to gain buy-in and support for the strategy.
- **Share impact stories:** Communicate the ROI analysis findings and ongoing performance updates to relevant stakeholders. Use clear and concise reporting formats to convey the impact of the strategy on business outcomes.
- **Engage stakeholders in dialogue:** Facilitate open discussions about the implications of the ROI analysis and

any recommended course corrections. Don't leave data up to individual interpretation. Refer to Chapter One about the importance of centering employee voice.

Additional Tips

- **Consider intangible benefits:** Not all benefits can be easily quantified. For example, a new marketing campaign might improve brand awareness, even if it's difficult to directly measure ROI.
- **Set a realistic timeframe:** ROI takes time to materialize, so set realistic expectations for when you expect to see a return. We have several case studies at thewinwinworkplace.com where you can find cross-sector examples for each Win-Win workplace pillar.

By following this six-step process, you can develop a solid approach to measuring the ROI of the Win-Win workplace strategies. This will help you make informed decisions about resource allocation and track the success of your initiative.

INTERPRETATION AND ACTIONABLE INSIGHTS

Imagine you've invested in creating a Win-Win workplace and a company culture that fuels employee thriving and business success. How do you know it's paying off? That's where Win-Win workplace ROI analysis comes in. It's like a translator, turning the positive impact of your company culture into numbers that business executives understand.

The ROI tells you if your Win-Win workplace initiatives are paying off. Positive results mean happy employees are translating into a healthier bottom line. Look for connections between your programs and improved metrics like productivity or lower turnover. But what if the numbers aren't so rosy? A negative ROI is a signal to investigate—your programs might need some tweaking. Don't get discouraged by a neutral ROI, either. It might mean you need more data or some fine-tuning to maximize the impact. Remember, company culture is a garden, and gardens take time to flourish.

FINDING THE SUCCESS STORIES AND WHAT NEEDS WORK

The ROI is like a spotlight, helping you identify areas where your efforts are shining. Maybe a new wellness program has boosted employee morale and lowered healthcare costs. Perhaps flexible work arrangements have led to happier, more productive teams. On the flip side, the ROI can also reveal areas that need some TLC. Are there programs with low participation? Are certain metrics not showing improvement? Dig into these areas to understand why they're falling short.

TURNING INSIGHTS INTO ACTION

Now comes the exciting part—using your ROI to grow your thriving workplace even further. Think of it as fertilizer for your company culture garden, which can be nurtured further by the following actions:

- **Feed the successes:** Programs with a positive ROI deserve a boost! Allocate more resources to these initiatives to keep them flourishing.
- **Revitalize what's struggling:** Some programs might need a makeover. Use employee feedback and pilot programs to refine them and get them back on track.

- **Align your garden with the big picture:** Make sure your thriving workplace initiatives are helping your entire company blossom. Ensure your company culture supports your overall business goals—a thriving and healthy workforce is the foundation for achieving them.

The key is to consistently measure and analyze your ROI. It's like checking on your garden regularly. By understanding the results, you can make informed decisions to cultivate a thriving workplace that fuels your company's success for years to come.

TELLING YOUR THRIVING WORKPLACE ROI STORY

After the hard work of measuring your thriving workplace ROI, it's time to share the story! But how do you translate data points into a compelling narrative that resonates with different audiences? Here's how to effectively communicate your ROI findings.

Presenting ROI Findings in a Clear and Compelling Manner

- **Focus on the "why" and the "so what":** Don't just present numbers—explain what they mean for the company. Connect ROI results to tangible benefits like increased productivity, improved customer satisfaction, or reduced turnover.
- **Visual storytelling:** Use charts, graphs, and infographics to make complex data easy to understand. Visually highlight key findings and trends to capture attention.
- **Keep it concise and clear:** Tailor the level of detail to your audience. Avoid jargon and technical terms—focus on a clear, impactful message.

Communicating the Value Proposition to Different Stakeholders

In sharing the insights and outcomes of the Win-Win workplace, it is critical to center the individual that you are aiming to inform—and, ideally, enroll as a champion of the new transformation. Tailoring communication to different stakeholders is crucial for maximizing engagement by addressing their specific interests, fostering better understanding through appropriate levels of detail, building stronger relationships through targeted messaging, and ultimately achieving better decision-making by ensuring everyone has the information they need in a way that resonates with them. The three primary stakeholders will be leadership, employees, and external partners. Here is a breakdown of each:

- **Leadership:** They'll be interested in the big picture—the overall impact of thriving workplace initiatives on the bottom line. Highlight the ROI's contribution to strategic goals and future growth.
- **Employees:** Focus on how thriving workplace initiatives contribute to their well-being and job satisfaction. Show how these programs translate to a more positive and productive work environment.
- **External partners:** For investors or potential clients, emphasize the ROI as a sign of a healthy, engaged workforce, leading to improved product quality and customer service.

Engaging Stakeholders in Discussions

- **Open a two-way dialogue:** Don't just present findings. Encourage questions and discussion. Use the ROI data as a springboard for brainstorming future strategies.

- **Address concerns proactively:** If the ROI isn't overwhelmingly positive, acknowledge any challenges and outline plans for improvement.
- **Celebrate successes:** Recognize and reward employees and teams who have contributed to the positive ROI.

By crafting a clear, compelling narrative and tailoring your communication to different stakeholders, you can turn your thriving workplace's ROI data into a powerful tool for engagement. This fosters a sense of shared purpose and commitment to continuously improve your company culture, ultimately driving long-term success.

CONTINUOUS IMPROVEMENT

Imagine your implementation of the selected Win-Win workplace pillar as a well-oiled machine. It's running smoothly, but there is always room for fine-tuning. That's the essence of Continuous Improvement (CI)—a philosophy that views progress as a never-ending journey. It's not about drastic overhauls but about constantly seeking small improvements that, over time, lead to significant gains.

But how do you measure those improvements? That's where ROI comes in again. It's the puzzle piece that allows you to quantify the impact of your CI efforts. Contiguously integrating ROI measurement into your performance evaluation processes is key. It helps you understand which adjustments are truly making a difference and which might need a rethink.

Think of it like this: You implement a new training program to improve customer service. By tracking metrics like customer satisfaction scores and sales figures, you can calculate the ROI of the program. Did it lead to happier customers and increased sales? If so, that's a win! But if the numbers aren't budging, it's time to gather feedback and iterate on your strategy.

This is where the magic of CI happens. Using the insights from ROI data and centering employee voice, you can refine your approach. Maybe the training program needs a different format, or perhaps it's targeting the wrong area altogether. By iterating on your strategies based on data and feedback, you ensure your CI efforts are constantly moving the needle in the right direction.

The goal of CI is to foster a culture of data-driven decision-making and accountability. When everyone in the organization—from leadership to frontline employees—understands the power of data and takes ownership of continuous improvement, it becomes a collective effort. This shared responsibility ensures that everyone is invested in seeking out inefficiencies and identifying ways to work smarter, not harder.

Imagine a team empowered to analyze their workflow and suggest streamlining processes. Or a department manager who uses data to identify areas for employee skill development. By fostering this culture, CI becomes more than a top-down initiative; it becomes a way of life, propelling your organization toward sustained success. Remember, CI is a continuous cycle: measure, analyze, refine, and repeat. It's through this ongoing process that you can unlock the true potential of your organization and create a thriving environment where everyone is empowered to contribute to lasting improvement.

REAPING THE REWARDS OF A WIN-WIN WORKPLACE

T hroughout *The Win-Win Workplace: How Thriving Employees Drive Bottom-Line Success*, we have delved into the strategies fostering an environment where both employees and organizations can flourish. As we reflect on the transformations that the profiled companies and leaders have undergone, alongside the journey you've made as a reader, I trust that it has become evident—indeed, *proven* by data—that cultivating a thriving workplace offers significant rewards.

From centering employee voices to embracing transparency about human capital, each chapter lit the way to creating a workplace where individuals thrive, and organizations prosper. Amid the myriad challenges and dynamic landscapes of modern business, the significance of crafting a Win-Win workplace cannot be overstated and is more important than at any other time in our history. Like the new landscape of work that emerged after the Great Depression, we are now facing a new world order of work that is the aftereffect of the pandemic. Seismic shifts are taking place in the future of work, and strategies and workplaces of Zero-Sum thinking risk not only their profitability but their very existence. We have seen how entrenched players in the past have missed key shifts in customer and employee behavior, from Blockbuster to Netflix, MTV to Apple Music streaming, and Sears to Walmart. The shift to the Win-Win workplace is the calling of our time. Those companies and leaders who are not on board risk being left with an empty shell, just like the Kenosha, Wisconsin, Chrysler Motors plant of my childhood. They played the Zero-Sum game and lost.

Beyond mere rhetoric, *The Win-Win Workplace* sets forth the nine pillars that comprise the foundation upon which organizational success and sustainable growth are built. It's a commitment to fostering an ecosystem where employees feel valued, empowered, and inspired, ultimately catalyzing innovation, productivity, and collective achievement.

As you embark on the journey to a thriving workplace, it's essential to acknowledge and celebrate the strides made thus far. From incremental improvements to monumental shifts in culture and mindset, each step forward is testament to the collective dedication to a workplace where bottom lines are lifted when all workers at all levels thrive.

In commemorating achievements and milestones reached, we pay homage to the dedication, resilience, and ingenuity exhibited by individuals and organizations alike. Whether it be the implementation of intersectional inclusion strategies or the reimagining of employee benefits, each accomplishment serves as a catalyst for further progress and inspiration for the journey ahead.

REWARDING WIN-WIN LEADERS WHO LIVE THESE VALUES

The people I call "Win-Win leaders" are the harbingers of the future. They fearlessly embrace challenges as opportunities for growth. They inspire team members by example to elevate themselves. They push an ethos of collaboration instead of competition.

Win-Win leaders aren't just people. A growth leader can be the courageous company that flattens its hierarchical structure, hires STARs, and lets employees determine the contours of their benefits packages. Although we refer to a Win-Win leader as the individual—a key figure such as a department head, team leader, or colleague who spearheads a Win-Win culture, leads by example, and fosters both personal and professional development—it is important to recognize that the visionary power of the prime mover doesn't have to come from just one person.

A Win-Win leader strives to see each person as an individual, not as a cog in service to a corporate end. A Win-Win leader sees each person as an opportunity to practice self-reflection and empathy. A Win-Win leader is constrained not by existing systems but by the limits of their imagination. A Win-Win leader is open about their successes, their failures, and their goals. A Win-Win leader takes time to water the seedlings around them and sees opportunity instead of deficit. In short, a Win-Win leader is the embodiment of optimism, agency, and mutualism.

For a Win-Win workplace to be realized, we need Win-Win leaders committed at all levels, from the front lines to the C-suite. Workplace transformation at the levels we've discussed requires a fundamental mindset shift around how we think about work and its purpose in our lives. It no longer has to be seen as mere transaction: I trade my hour of time for an hour's wage in a paycheck. A workplace can be a place of community learning and, yes, for finding one's passion and raison d'être!

Kerry's Story, Revisited

Remember Kerry Siggins from Chapter Nine? She was a beneficiary of an employer, StoneAge, that eschewed traditional structures and ideologies, instead fashioning its organization, policy, and mindset in such a way that Kerry—and all of its employees—could feel seen, valued, and included as part of the future for the company. Kerry, in turn, invested in the company's mission and embraced its values as her own, leaving her feeling more fulfilled than ever before.

Being able to grow inside that structure primed Kerry to be a Win-Win leader who pushed StoneAge to an even closer alignment of its business and its values. She continued further up the path to an employee-centered culture, growing existing programs, and fostering existing talent. She listened to those around her and elevated those below her, giving every member of her company a voice, even as the company undertook expansion.

As Kerry's example shows, centering the individual members that make an organization work results in both personal and professional transformations. From being lost, battling addiction, and wounded, Kerry found a workplace that encouraged her to bring her best self to work every day—and saw potential she could not see in herself. Her company's leadership allowed her to align herself with the product of her labor, sharing in her hard work and celebrating the hard work of others. StoneAge became more of a community than a company—more of a group of members than employees.

By embracing work-life synergy, businesses unlock the potential for increased employee engagement, creativity, and ultimately, enhanced profitability. By promoting authenticity, businesses cultivate a stronger sense of belonging, motivation, and loyalty among their workforce, driving productivity and profitability. By embracing the whole life equation, businesses can create a thriving ecosystem where people and profitability go hand in hand.

By embracing Kerry, StoneAge gave Kerry meaning; she then grew and passed the meaning along. She became a Win-Win leader, nurturing the next generation of Win-Win leaders.

STARTING WITH METRICS: THE FOUNDATION OF SUCCESS

Building a Win-Win workplace necessitates a data-driven approach, underpinned by the identification and alignment of key metrics with organizational goals. By meticulously measuring the impact of Win-Win workplace strategies, organizations can ascertain progress, identify areas for improvement, and make informed decisions to cultivate an environment conducive to sustained success. Employee well-being and ROI in the Win-Win workplace are inextricably linked.

ALIGNING METRICS WITH STRATEGY AND GOALS

Aligning key metrics with the nine Win-Win workplace pillars outlined in this book is essential. Establishing these metrics at the outset, or embedding them early in the process, ensures they are integral to evaluating progress. Many people mistakenly believe that metrics are something to be set up at the end to evaluate results. However, waiting until the end means missing out on critical data and insights throughout the process. By setting up metrics from the beginning, you create a framework that allows you to measure and guide your strategic initiatives in real time.

From centering employee voices to distributing leadership and creating structures where every worker can grow into leadership and contribute meaningfully through their entrepreneurial mindsets, each strategy needs to be accompanied by a set of measurable indicators for quantifying progress. This proactive approach ensures that you can track and drive your strategic goals effectively from the start, rather than scrambling to measure success after the fact. Starting with metrics helps not only in assessing progress but also in making informed decisions and adjustments along the way, ultimately leading to more successful and sustainable outcomes.

WHERE TO START: A CALL TO ACTION

This book covers a vast array of strategies through its nine Win-Win workplace pillars, which can seem overwhelming to implement all at once. It's crucial to recognize that you don't need to tackle everything simultaneously. Begin by centering employee voices—this is the foundation. Listen to what your employees are saying, understand their needs, and identify where you have the most energy and support within your organization.

Next, consider the specific challenges you're facing. Is your primary issue retention? Culture? Identify your most pressing problems and start there. Align your metrics with these initial focus areas. Form a team that will help you collect data, pilot new initiatives, and evaluate the results. Remember, you don't need to follow the pillars in a strict order; go where you see opportunities for immediate improvement.

YOU'VE GOT THIS!

Creating a thriving workplace might seem like a lofty goal, but the strategies outlined in this book are practical and achievable, regardless of your company size or industry. Remember, even small improvements in employee well-being and engagement can translate into significant ROI benefits. Think happier, more productive employees leading to higher customer satisfaction, increased innovation, and ultimately, a stronger bottom line. It's a Win-Win for everyone involved.

By taking action and fostering a collaborative environment, you can inspire others to join you on this journey. Remember, building a thriving workplace is an investment in your most valuable asset—people. The rewards are substantial, not just for you, your peers and your employees, but for your entire organization's success. So, take a deep breath, embrace the potential, and get ready to create a workplace where everyone flourishes!

LOOKING AHEAD—AND AROUND THE CORNER

Creating a thriving workplace is an ongoing journey. I encourage you to stay committed to continuous improvement and innovation. To know that you are reading this book and have gotten to the conclusion gives me optimism for the future of work and for Win-Win workplaces around the world. I welcome you to share your experiences and insights with me and others at thewinwinworkplace.com. Join a community of like-minded individuals committed to creating thriving workplaces. You'll find case studies, research, templates, resources, and support for those embarking on their own workplace transformation journey at the same website.

Supporting readers like you is my life's calling. From growing up watching my grandfather find dignity at work, I know the power of a Win-Win workplace. I am extremely grateful to you for your engagement and commitment. The book's purpose dovetails with my personal mission: to show that when we all—frontline employees, managers, executives, and policy makers—embrace a more equitable environment centered on trust, accountability, collaboration, and equity, *everyone* is better off. Creating a Win-Win workplace is within reach for all organizations. Now you have the blueprint. It is up to you to get started.

The Win-Win Workplace Discussion Guide

This Discussion Guide is crafted to foster insightful conversations among C-suite leaders, frontline leaders, and workers about the Win-Win workplace pillars that drive a successful and engaging work environment. It aims to facilitate reflection, discussion, and actionable insights, promoting a holistic approach to workplace improvement and employee well-being that translates into bottom-line success.

BENEFITS FOR STAKEHOLDERS

1. C-Suite Leaders

This guide empowers C-suite leaders in the following areas:

- **Strategically addressing employee needs:** Gain insights into employee feedback and experiences, enabling strategic adjustments that enhance engagement and performance.
- **Enhancing business outcomes:** Leverage feedback to refine initiatives that can positively impact profits, revenue, stock price, and asset valuation.
- **Driving organizational change:** Implement practices that align with employee values and needs, fostering a positive and productive work environment.

2. Frontline Leaders

This guide empowers frontline leaders in the following areas:

- **Improving team dynamics:** Use the tools to foster open communication, collaboration, and a supportive environment within their teams.
- **Effective leadership practices:** Implement the strategies to enhance management practices based on employee feedback and experiences.
- **Enhancing engagement:** Apply the techniques to increase team motivation and ownership, leading to better business outcomes.

3. Workers

This guide empowers workers in the following areas:

- **Provoking conversations:** Use the questions to initiate meaningful discussions with current employers about areas for improvement and feedback mechanisms.
- **Assessing future opportunities:** Apply the guide's questions as a lens to evaluate potential employers, ensuring alignment with their values and needs.
- **Influencing change:** Share their perspectives and suggestions, leading to actionable changes that enhance their workplace experience and job satisfaction.

Appendix A

The Nine Win-Win Workplace Pillars

The Nine Win-Win Workplace Pillars

Pillar	Stake-holder	Questions
One: Centering Employee Voices	C-suite leaders	• How do you currently gather actionable feedback from employees across the organization? • What steps are taken to ensure employee feedback is represented in strategic decisions? • Can you share examples where employee feedback directly contributed to a positive change and its impact on business outcomes?
	Frontline leaders	• How do you encourage your team to share their ideas and concerns? • What methods do you use to communicate the impact of their feedback back to them? • Can you share a time when an idea from your team led to a significant improvement in your operations?
	Workers	• Do you feel your voice is heard and valued in the company? Why or why not? • Can you recall an instance when your feedback was implemented, and what was the outcome? • What improvements would you suggest for the current feedback mechanisms?

(continued)

The Nine Win-Win Workplace Pillars (Continued)

Pillar	Stake-holder	Questions
Two: Cultivating Mutualistic Working Relationships	C-suite leaders	• How do you promote positive and collaborative relationships between employees and employers? • What initiatives have you introduced to align employee rewards with purpose and values? • How do you measure the impact of these initiatives on company performance?
	Frontline leaders	• How do you foster a sense of appreciation and contribution within your team? • Can you share examples of nonmonetary rewards you use to motivate your team? • What impact have you observed from these efforts on employee engagement and retention?
	Workers	• How do you feel about the level of connection and collaboration in your workplace? • What nonmonetary rewards do you find most motivating? • How do you feel your work aligns with your personal values and purpose?
Three: Implementing Intersectional Inclusion Strategies	C-suite leaders	• How does your organization support employees in bringing their authentic selves to work? • What strategies do you have in place to acknowledge and value diverse experiences?
	Frontline leaders	• How do you create an inclusive environment for your team members? • Can you share examples of how you support team members based on their intersectional identities? • What challenges have you faced in implementing inclusion strategies, and what training or other support did you receive to prepare you?

Pillar	Stake-holder	Questions
		• How do you ensure that the intersectional identities and diverse personal and work experiences employees bring are being strategically leveraged throughout the organization? Can you name 2 or 3 examples? Can your frontline leaders name an example?
	Workers	• Do you feel you can be your authentic self at work? Why or why not? • How does the company support your unique needs and background? • What changes would you suggest to better leverage the intersectional identities of yourself or your colleagues in the workplace?
Four: Reimagining Employee Benefits	C-suite leaders	• How do you decide which benefits to offer to meet diverse employee needs? • What innovative benefits have you introduced recently, and what has been their impact? • How do you measure employee satisfaction and loyalty related to benefits?
	Frontline leaders	• How do you communicate available benefits to your team? • How do you gather feedback on the effectiveness of current benefits? • Can you share an instance where a benefit suggestion from your team was implemented?
	Workers	• How satisfied are you with the current benefits offered by your company? • What additional benefits would you like to see, and why? • To what extent do you feel that you have the ability to influence the benefits offered?

(*continued*)

The Nine Win-Win Workplace Pillars (Continued)

Pillar	Stakeholder	Questions
Five: Activating Frontline Leaders	C-suite leaders	• How do you empower frontline leaders to champion employee inclusion initiatives? • What human-centered strategies have you implemented at the frontline manager level? • How do you support decision-making closer to the work being done?
	Frontline leaders	• How do you promote diversity, equity, inclusion, and justice within your team? • Can you share a successful human-centered strategy you implemented? • How do you involve your team in decision-making processes?
	Workers	• How do you perceive the efforts of your frontline managers to develop their skills as leaders of people? • Can you share an experience where you felt included in decision-making? • What support do you need from frontline managers to feel more engaged and responsible?
Six: Hiring STARs versus Prioritizing Credentials	C-suite leaders	• How do you prioritize skills and abilities over traditional credentials in your hiring process? • What innovative assessment methods have you developed to identify talent? • How has this approach impacted your talent pool and business outcomes?
	Frontline leaders	• How do you identify and support the development of skills within your team? • Can you share an example of a team member who thrived despite nontraditional credentials? • What challenges have you faced in shifting away from traditional hiring criteria?

Pillar	Stake-holder	Questions
	Workers	• How do you feel about the emphasis on skills and abilities over traditional credentials? • Have you experienced any opportunities due to this approach? • What skills or talents do you believe are undervalued in the current system?
Seven: Developing Deep Talent Benches	C-suite leaders	• What strategies do you use to nurture and grow talent within your organization? • How do you invest in training and development programs for your employees? • How do you measure the success of these programs in retaining top talent?
	Frontline leaders	• How do you identify potential future leaders within your team? • Can you share examples of how you've supported team members' career advancement? • What training and development opportunities do you offer to your team?
	Workers	• Do you feel there are clear pathways for career advancement in your company? • How have training and development programs helped you in your role? • What additional support do you need to advance your career?
Eight: Using Human-Capital Reporting as a Competitive Strategy	C-suite leaders	• How do you use data and metrics related to employees to inform strategic decision-making? • What human capital data do you track and measure, and how do you communicate this to employees? • How has increased transparency impacted employee trust and company performance?

(continued)

The Nine Win-Win Workplace Pillars (Continued)

Pillar	Stakeholder	Questions
Eight (continued)	Frontline leaders	• How do you incorporate human capital data into your management practices? • Can you share examples of how transparency in decision-making has benefited your team? • What challenges have you faced in increasing transparency, and how did you address them?
	Workers	• How transparent do you feel the company is about decisions affecting employees? • How does knowing human capital data impact your trust in the company? • What additional information would you like to have about the company's decision-making process?
Nine: Distributing Leadership via Entrepreneurial Structures	C-suite leaders	• How do you empower employees at all levels to share ideas and make decisions? • What structures have you implemented to move beyond rigid hierarchies? • How do you measure the impact of these structures on collaboration and innovation?
	Frontline leaders	• How do you encourage team members to take ownership and share their expertise? • Can you share examples of successful ideas that came from nonleadership employees? • What challenges have you faced in implementing flatter organizational structures?
	Workers	• How empowered do you feel to share your ideas and take ownership of decisions? • Can you share an instance where your idea was implemented and describe its impact? • What support do you need to feel more confident in contributing to decision-making?

Appendix B

Facilitator Guide

This Facilitator Guide is designed to guide discussions around the key themes of *The Win-Win Workplace* and facilitate a deeper understanding of how to create a more employee-centric and successful organization. Its target audience is leaders, managers, human resources professionals, and employees from various levels within an organization.

OBJECTIVES

- Foster open and honest dialogue about workplace culture and employee experiences.
- Generate actionable insights and strategies for improving employee well-being and organizational performance.
- Build a shared understanding of the importance of a Win-Win approach to workplace relationships.

PREPARATION

- Read the book thoroughly and familiarize yourself with the key concepts and arguments.
- Review the Discussion Guide and prepare additional questions or activities as needed.
- Consider the group size and dynamics and adjust the facilitation style accordingly.
- Create a welcoming and inclusive atmosphere for participants to share their thoughts and experiences.

FACILITATION TIPS

- Encourage active participation from all participants.
- Balance listening and speaking time among group members.
- Summarize key points and identify common themes.
- Use visual aids or props to enhance engagement.
- Be prepared to handle sensitive topics with empathy and respect.

Pillar One: Centering Employee Voices

- How does a culture of silence impact innovation and problem-solving within your organization?
- What technology tools can be used to gather and analyze employee feedback more effectively?
- How can leaders ensure that employee feedback is not just heard but acted upon?

Pillar Two: Cultivating Mutualistic Working Relationships

- How does a strong sense of community impact employee engagement and productivity?
- What specific actions can leaders take to foster a culture of appreciation and recognition?
- How can organizations measure the ROI of initiatives focused on human connection?

Pillar Three: Implementing Intersectional Inclusion Strategies

- What steps can organizations take to create an authentic workplace where employees don't feel pressured to mask their identities?
- Which current workplace structures and policies could be reimagined through an intersectional lens to better support diverse identities?

- How can leveraging intersectional identities drive business success, and what benefits might this offer in innovation, customer engagement, and competitiveness?

Pillar Four: Reimagining Employee Benefits

- How can involving employees in recommending and shaping their own benefits contribute to increased job satisfaction and loyalty, and what impact might this have on the company's overall financial performance?
- What innovative benefits can organizations offer to meet the diverse needs of their workforce?
- How does financial well-being impact overall employee well-being and job performance?

Pillar Five: Activating Frontline Leaders

- What specific challenges do frontline leaders face in creating a positive work environment?
- How can organizations provide frontline leaders with the training and resources they need to succeed?
- How can providing improved onboarding and training support for frontline managers improve employee experience and business success?

Pillar Six: Hiring STARs versus Prioritizing Credentials

- How can organizations identify and assess the skills and competencies needed for future success?
- What alternative assessment methods can be used to evaluate potential employees?
- How can organizations build a talent pipeline through apprenticeships and internships?

Pillar Seven: Developing Deep Talent Benches

- What role does leadership development play in creating a high-performance culture?
- How can organizations foster a culture of continuous learning and development?
- How can employees be empowered to take ownership of their career growth?

Pillar Eight: Using Human-Capital Reporting as a Competitive Strategy

- How can organizations effectively use human capital data, such as compensation, training, and well-being metrics, to inform strategic decision-making and communicate these factors transparently to employees?
- What are best practices for tracking human capital data, and how can transparency boost employee trust?
- How can data-driven decision-making and better workforce planning enhance profits, revenue, and asset valuation?

Pillar Nine: Distributing Leadership via Entrepreneurial Structures

- How can organizations empower employees to make decisions at the local level?
- What structures and processes can support a more decentralized approach to management?
- How can organizations measure the impact of employee-driven initiatives?

Additional Activities

- **Case study analysis:** Present a case study of a company featured in *The Win-Win Workplace* to demonstrate how they successfully implemented Win-Win workplace practices.

- **Role-playing:** Simulate challenging workplace scenarios and practice effective communication and problem-solving skills.
- **Action planning:** Encourage participants to develop specific action plans to implement the ideas discussed.

By following this Facilitator Guide and incorporating the provided discussion questions, you can create engaging and productive conversations that lead to positive change within any organization.

Notes

Introduction

1. "Employment Situation Summary—2024 M02 Results," US Bureau of Labor Statistics, March 8, 2024, https://www.bls.gov/news.release/empsit.nr0.htm.
2. Jim Mateja, "Chrysler Closing Kenosha Plant," *Chicago Tribune*, August 8, 2021, https://www.chicagotribune.com/1988/01/28/chrysler-closing-kenosha-plant/.
3. Jenna Jacobs, "American Motors," in *Encyclopedia of Milwaukee*, accessed September 12, 2024, https://emke.uwm.edu/entry/american-motors/.
4. "State of the Global Workplace: From Suffering to Thriving," Gallup.com, accessed June 13, 2024, https://www.gallup.com/workplace/349484/state-of-the-global-workplace.aspx?thank-you-report-form=1.
5. Randstad, *Workmonitor 2023: Flexible but Stable*, 2023, https://workforceinsights.randstad.com/hubfs/Workmonitor/2023/Randstad_Workmonitor_2023.pdf?hsLang=nl.
6. Loh-Sze Leung and Nancy Snyder, *Taking Action: Positioning Low-Income Workers to Succeed in a Changing Economy*, August 2019, https://assets.aecf.org/m/resourcedoc/hatcher-takingaction-2019.pdf.
7. Bobby Allyn, "Nearly 25,000 Tech Workers Were Laid Off in the First Weeks of 2024. Why Is That?," *NPR*, January 28, 2024, https://www.npr.org/2024/01/28/1227326215/nearly-25-000-tech-workers-laid-off-in-the-first-weeks-of-2024-whats-going-on.
8. Angela Jackson, "Grand Challenge to Reinvent Workforce Development," in *Workforce Realigned: How New Partnerships Are Advancing Economic Mobility*, ed. Social Finance, Federal Reserve Bank of Atlanta, and Federal Reserve Bank of Philadelphia (Boston, MA: Social Finance, 2021), 168–185.
9. Allyn, "Nearly 25,000 Tech Workers Were Laid Off"; Angela Jackson, "Grads of Life Brandvoice: The Social Determinants of Work," *Forbes*, August 26, 2021, https://www.forbes.com/sites/gradsoflife/2021/08/26/the-social-determinants-of-work/.

Chapter 1

1. "The Great Gloom: In 2023, Employees Are Unhappier Than Ever. Why?," BambooHR, accessed June 1, 2024, https://www.bamboohr.com/resources /guides/employee-happiness-h1-2023?utm_source=newswire&amp%3Butm _medium=press+release&amp%3Butm_campaign=Q2%2723.
2. Jim Harter, "Percent Who Feel Employer Cares about Their Wellbeing Plummets," Gallup.com, March 18, 2022, https://www.gallup.com/workplace/390776 /percent-feel-employer-cares-wellbeing-plummets.aspx.
3. "How to Improve Employee Engagement in the Workplace," Gallup.com, accessed May 30, 2024, https://www.gallup.com/workplace/285674/improve -employee-engagement-workplace.aspx#ite-357638.
4. Peter Stavros, email message to author, June 25, 2024.

Chapter 2

1. Sandra Sobieraj Westfall, interview by Angela Jackson, July 18, 2024.
2. Jessica Howington, "Toxic Managers and Coworkers Pervasive in the Workplace," *FlexJobs Blog*, September 18, 2023, https://www.flexjobs.com/blog /post/toxic-managers-coworkers-make-toxic-workplace/.
3. Howington, "Toxic Managers"; Rose Hunt, "93% of UK Employees Have Experienced a 'Toxic Workplace', Study Finds," Gleeson Recruitment Group, archived September 28, 2022, at the Wayback Machine, https://web.archive .org/web/20220928194204/https://www.workwithglee.com/blog/2022/07 /93-percent-of-uk-employees-have-experienced-a-toxic-workplace-study -finds/.
4. Nectar Gan, "Chinese Tech Exec's Fiery Endorsement of Toxic Workplace Culture Sparks Backlash—and Costs Her Job," *Yahoo! Finance*, May 9, 2024, https://finance.yahoo.com/news/bosses-thinking-baidu-pr-chief-115050444 .html.
5. Waiyee Yip, "China Steps In to Regulate Brutal '996' Work Culture," *BBC News*, September 1, 2021, https://www.bbc.com/news/world-asia-china -58381538.
6. Caitlin Rosenthal, "Plantations Practiced Modern Management," *Harvard Business Review*, September 2013, https://hbr.org/2013/09/plantations-practiced -modern-management.
7. Caitlin Rosenthal, *Accounting for Slavery: Masters and Management* (Cambridge, MA: Harvard University Press, 2019).
8. Sebastian Buck, "The Business Case for Investing in Employee Well-Being," *Fast Company*, May 23, 2023, https://www.fastcompany.com/90899166/the -business-case-for-investing-in-employee-well-being.
9. Jim Harter, "Percent Who Feel Employer Cares about Their Wellbeing Plummets," Gallup.com, March 18, 2022, https://www.gallup.com/workplace /390776/percent-feel-employer-cares-wellbeing-plummets.aspx.
10. Kathryn Mayer, "Most Workers Say Paychecks Aren't Keeping Up with Inflation," SHRM, March 1, 2024, https://www.shrm.org/topics-tools/news/benefits -compensation/inflation-toll-employee-paychecks-american-staffing -association#:~:text=More%20than%20half%20of%20workers,About%20 2%2C000%20workers%20were%20surveyed.

11. E. Napoletano, "15 Companies That Help Pay Off Student Loans," *U.S. News*, June 5, 2024, https://money.usnews.com/loans/student-loans/articles/companies-that-help-pay-off-student-loans; Kimpton Hotels & Restaurants, "Kimpton Hotels & Restaurants Partners with Talkspace to Provide Licensed Therapy to Guests and Employees," press release, February 23, 2022, https://www.ihg.com/kimptonhotels/content/us/es/press/releases/kimpton-hotels-restaurants-partners-wth-talkspace-to-provide-licensed-therapy-to-guests-and-employees.

12. "Indicators: Employee Wellbeing," Gallup.com, accessed June 12, 2024, https://www.gallup.com/394424/indicator-employee-wellbeing.aspx.

13. Shane McFeely and Ben Wigert, "This Fixable Problem Costs U.S. Businesses \$1 Trillion," Gallup.com, March 13, 2019, https://www.gallup.com/workplace/247391/fixable-problem-costs-businessestrillion.aspx#:~:text=The%20cost%20of%20replacing%20an,to%20%24Fa%20million%20per%20year.

14. Charlotte Fritz, YoungAh Park, and Brittnie R. Shepherd, "Workplace Incivility Ruins My Sleep and Yours: The Costs of Being in a Work-Linked Relationship," *Occupational Health Science* 3, no. 1 (March 1, 2019): 1–21.

15. Jesse Stanchak, "The Hidden Costs of Incivility in the Workplace," SHRM, May 14, 2024, https://www.shrm.org/executive-network/insights/the-hidden-costs-of-incivility-in-the-workplace.

16. Jerry Greenfield, email correspondence with Angela Jackson, June 6, 2024.

17. "Fairtrade," Ben & Jerry's, June 9, 2023, https://www.benjerry.com/values/issues-we-care-about/fairtrade.

18. "Fairtrade."

19. Jobina Gonsalves, interview by Angela Jackson, April 14, 2023.

20. P. J. Zak, "The Neuroscience of High-Trust Organizations," *Consulting Psychology Journal* 70, no. 1 (2018): 441–445.

21. Jimmy Nesbitt, "Ben & Jerry's and Burlington Scoop Shop Workers Reach First Contract Agreement," *VTDigger*, January 18, 2019, https://vtdigger.org/2024/01/18/ben-jerrys-and-burlington-scoop-shop-workers-reach-first-contract-agreement/.

22. Nesbitt, "Ben & Jerry's."

23. "Ben and Jerry's Homemade Overview," PitchBook, accessed September 11, 2024, https://my.pitchbook.com/profile/95759-83/.

Chapter 3

1. Sundiatu Dixon-Fyle, Kevin Dolan, Dame Vivian Hunt, and Sara Prince, "Diversity Wins: How Inclusion Matters," McKinsey & Company, May 19, 2020, https://www.mckinsey.com/featured-insights/diversity-and-inclusion/diversity-wins-how-inclusion-matters.

2. Kimberlé Crenshaw, "Demarginalizing the Intersection of Race and Sex: A Black Feminist Critique of Antidiscrimination Doctrine, Feminist Theory and Antiracist Politics," *University of Chicago Legal Forum* (1989): 139–167.

3. Geneva Richards, interview by Angela Jackson, February 7, 2021.

4. International Labor Organization, *Care Work and Care Jobs for the Future of Decent Work* (Geneva: International Labor Organization, 2018), 31.

5. Feeding America, *The Impact of the Coronavirus on Food Insecurity in 2020 and 2021*, March 2021, https://www.feedingamerica.org/sites/default/files/2021 -03/National%20Projections%20Brief_3.9.2021_0.pdf; Elaine Waxman, Julio Salas, Poonam Gupta, and Michael Karpman, "Food Insecurity Trended Upward in Midst of High Inflation and Fewer Supports: Findings from the Health Reform Monitoring Survey, June 2022," Urban Institute, September 2022, https://www.urban.org/sites/default/files/2022-09/HRMS%20Food%20 Insecurity%20Brief_0.pdf.

6. Bruce D. Meyer, Angela Wyse, Alexa Grunwaldt, Carla Medalia, and Derek Wu, "Learning about Homelessness Using Linked Survey and Administrative Data," Working Paper 28861, National Bureau of Economic Research, May 31, 2021, https://www.nber.org/papers/w28861.

7. World Health Organization, *The World Health Report 2001: Mental Health: New Understanding, New Hope*, 2001, https://iris.who.int/bitstream/handle /10665/42390/WHR_2001.pdf?sequence=1&isAllowed=y.

8. Erica Coe, Jenny Cordina, Kana Enomoto, Raelyn Jacobson, Sharon Mei, and Nikhil Seshan, "Addressing the Unprecedented Behavioral-Health Challenges Facing Generation Z," McKinsey & Company, January 14, 2022, https://www.mckinsey.com/industries/healthcare/our-insights/addressing-the -unprecedented-behavioral-health-challenges-facing-generation-z; Jonathan Haidt, *The Anxious Generation: How the Great Rewiring of Childhood Is Causing an Epidemic of Mental Illness* (New York: Penguin, 2024).

9. Jordan Turner, "Employees Seek Personal Value and Purpose at Work. Be Prepared to Deliver," Gartner, March 29, 2023, https://www.gartner.com/en /articles/employees-seek-personal-value-and-purpose-at-work-be-prepared-to -deliver.

10. Turner, "Employees Seek Personal Value."

11. "Transportation Economic Trends: Transportation Spending—Average Household," Bureau of Transportation Statistics, accessed July 28, 2024, https://data .bts.gov/stories/s/Transportation-Economic-Trends-Transportation-Spen/ida7 -k95k/.

12. Rukmini Callimachi and Ruth Fremson, "I Live in My Car," *New York Times*, October 17, 2023, https://www.nytimes.com/2023/10/17/realestate /car-homeless-rent-debt-mortgage.html?searchResultPosition=5.

13. Korayem Razik, "Presenteeism Costs 10x More Than Absenteeism. How Can Leaders Tackle This?," *Thrive Global*, January 14, 2021, https://community .thriveglobal.com/presenteeism-costs-10x-more-than-absenteeism-how -can-leaders-tackle-this/#:~:text=The%20High%20Cost%20of%20 Presenteeism,based%20on%20the%20BLS%20data.

14. Razik, "Presenteeism Costs 10x More."

15. Razik, "Presenteeism Costs 10x More."

16. Razik, "Presenteeism Costs 10x More."

17. Razik, "Presenteeism Costs 10x More."

18. Yamini Rangan, CEO of HubSpot, interview by Caroline Hyde, *Bloomberg*, March 7, 2024, https://www.bloomberg.com/news/videos/2024-03-07/treat -company-culture-like-a-product-rangan-video.

19. Rangan interview.

20. Rangan interview.

21. Ellie Flanagan, "HubSpot's CEO Brian Halligan Injured in Accident; Expected to Make a Full and Complete Recovery," HubSpot, January 19, 2023, https://www.hubspot.com/company-news/hubspots-ceo-brian-halligan -injured-in-accident-expected-to-make-a-full-and-complete-recovery.

22. Sundiatu Dixon-Fyle, Kevin Dolan, Dame Vivian Hunt, and Sara Prince, "Diversity Wins: How Inclusion Matters," McKinsey & Company, May 19, 2020, https://www.mckinsey.com/featured-insights/diversity-and-inclusion/diversity -wins-how-inclusion-matters.

23. Robert D. Austin, and Gary P. Pisano, "Neurodiversity Is a Competitive Advantage," *Harvard Business Review*, August 27, 2021, https://hbr.org/2017/05 /neurodiversity-as-a-competitive-advantage.

24. Abayomi Olusunle, "Neurodiversity and Leadership: How to Create a Diverse and Inclusive Executive Team," World Economic Forum, August 22, 2023, https://www.weforum.org/agenda/2023/08/neurodiversity-how-to-create -inclusive-leadership-team/?utm_content=23%2F08%2F2023%2B17%3A45 &utm_medium=social_scheduler&utm_source=linkedin&utm_term =Better%2BBusiness.

25. Olusunle, "Neurodiversity and Leadership."

26. Olusunle, "Neurodiversity and Leadership."

27. Dixon-Fyle et al., "Diversity Wins."

Chapter 4

1. Vickie Braden, interview by Angela Jackson, March 1, 2022.

2. Rachel Romer, conversation with author, April 12, 2023.

3. Bonnie Rochman, "Viewpoint: How Yahoo CEO Marissa Mayer Is Building a Nursery by Her Office, and Dissing Working Moms," *Time*, February 28, 2013, https://healthland.time.com/2013/02/28/how-yahoo-ceo-marissa-mayer-is -building-a-nursery-by-her-office-and-dissing-working-moms/.

4. Rachel Romer, email to Guild Staff, 2018.

5. Alexandra Wilson, "This Tech Unicorn Just Opened a Million-Dollar Daycare, as Companies Fight to Retain Female Talent," *Forbes*, April 22, 2021, https://www.forbes.com/sites/alexandrawilson1/2021/04/22/this-tech -unicorn-just-opened-a-million-dollar-daycare-as-companies-fight-to-retain -female-talent/.

6. In 2023, Rachel Romer experienced a health event and stepped down from her role as CEO. I deeply respect her leadership and wish her strength in her recovery.

7. Sam Ryan, Cofounder of Zeelo, interview by Angela Jackson, June 7, 2023.

8. Zeelo, "As part of Tesco's Red Door platform in 2021, we introduced a trusted, efficient, and cost-effective shuttle program for shift workers. Fast forward three years and we are delighted to see how Zeelo continues to make a real impact; improving the commuting experience for Tesco employees in its Goole location," Facebook, June 3, 2024, https://www.facebook.com/gozeelo/videos /838003114479511/.

9. Zeelo, "As part of Tesco's."

10. Sam Ryan, email to author, July 3, 2024.

11. Sam Ryan, email to author, July 3, 2024.

Chapter 5

1. Quy Huy, "In Praise of Middle Managers," *Harvard Business Review*, August 1, 2014, https://hbr.org/2001/09/in-praise-of-middle-managers.

2. David Brooks, "The Quiet Magic of Middle Managers," *New York Times*, April 11, 2024, https://www.nytimes.com/2024/04/11/opinion/middle-managers-business-society.html.

3. Sarah Pakstis, "The Importance of Developing Your Frontline Leaders," *Harvard Business Publishing Blog*, August 24, 2020, https://www.harvardbusiness.org/the-importance-of-developing-your-frontline-leaders; Ron Ashkenas, "First-Time Managers, Don't Do Your Team's Work for Them," *Harvard Business Review*, September 21, 2015, https://hbr.org/2015/09/first-time-managers-dont-do-your-teams-work-for-them.

4. Chartered Management Institute, "New Study: Bad Managers and Toxic Work Culture Causing One in Three Staff to Walk," press release, October 16, 2023, https://www.managers.org.uk/about-cmi/media-centre/press-releases/bad-managers-and-toxic-work-culture-causing-one-in-three-staff-to-walk/.

5. Brooks Holtom, Terence Mitchell, Thomas Lee, and Marion Eberly, "5 Turnover and Retention Research: A Glance at the Past, a Closer Review of the Present, and a Venture into the Future," *Academy of Management Annals* 2, no. 1 (2008): 231–274; "The Benefits of Employee Engagement," Gallup.com, May 16, 2024, https://www.gallup.com/workplace/236927/employee-engagement-drives-growth.aspx.

6. Diane Belcher, "Leadership Development Gaps among Frontline Leaders—Harvard," *Harvard Business Publishing Blog*, April 21, 2023, https://www.harvardbusiness.org/frontline-leaders-are-hungry-for-development-can-organizations-deliver/.

7. PrismWork, *RESET: Men, Leadership, and the New World of Work*, March 2, 2023, https://modernleadership4men.com.

8. PrismWork, *RESET*.

9. Emily Field, Alexis Krivkovich, Sandra Kügele, Nicole Robinson, and Lareina Yee, "Women in the Workplace 2023," McKinsey & Company, October 5, 2023, https://www.mckinsey.com/featured-insights/diversity-and-inclusion/women-in-the-workplace; World Economic Forum, *Global Gender Gap Report 2023*, June 20, 2023, https://www3.weforum.org/docs/WEF_GGGR_2023.pdf.

10. Lisen Stromberg, Founder of PrismWork, interview by Angela Jackson, May 24, 2024.

11. "Our Mission," Empower Work, accessed July 14, 2024, https://www.empowerwork.org/about-us.

12. Anonymous, personal interview by Angela Jackson, March 1, 20203 to June 28, 2023 (names withheld at interviewee's request).

13. "How to Improve Employee Engagement in the Workplace," Gallup.com, June 4, 2024, https://www.gallup.com/workplace/285674/improve-employee-engagement-workplace.aspx.

14. John Pitonyak and Rob Desimone, "How to Engage Frontline Managers," Gallup.com, August 9, 2022, https://www.gallup.com/workplace/395210/engage-frontline-managers.aspx.

15. Anonymous, personal interview by Angela Jackson, March 20, 2024 (name withheld at interviewee's request).

16. Brian Elliott, "It's Time to Free the Middle Manager," *Harvard Business Review*, May 21, 2021, https://hbr.org/2021/05/its-time-to-free-the-middle-manager.

17. Brian Elliott, "Hybrid Rules: The Emerging Playbook for Flexible Work," Future Forum, October 14, 2021, https://futureforum.com/2021/01/28/hybrid-rules-the-emerging-playbook-for-flexible-work/.

18. Elliott, "Hybrid Rules."

19. "Future of the Workforce," *The 19th*, November 18, 2022, https://19thnews.org/events/future-of-the-workforce-austin-texas/.

20. "Future of the Workforce," *The 19th*, November 18, 2022, https://19thnews.org/events/future-of-the-workforce-austin-texas/.

21. Stephen R. Covey, *The 7 Habits of Highly Effective People: Revised and Updated*, 30th ed. (New York: Simon & Schuster, n.d.), "Habit 4: Think Win-Win."

22. Michael Leimbach, "Leadership Development in the Age of the Great Resignation," *Training*, May 16, 2022, https://trainingmag.com/leadership-development-in-the-age-of-the-the-great-resignation/.

23. Leimbach, "Leadership Development."

24. Angela Jackson, "Win-Win People Leader Training: Building Effective Leaders Through Continuous Learning and Development," Future Forward Strategies, September 25, 2023.

25. Leimbach, "Leadership Development."

26. Anonymous, personal interview by Angela Jackson, June 28, 2023 (name withheld at interviewee's request).

Chapter 6

1. Mike Rosenbaum, Founder of Catalyte, interview by Angela Jackson, February 20, 2023.

2. Opportunity@Work, *Reach for the STARs: Realizing the Potential of America's Hidden Talent Pool*, 2020, https://opportunityatwork.org/our-solutions/stars-insights/reach-stars-report/.

3. Andrew Jack, "Employers Look to Rip the 'Paper Ceiling' for Non-Graduates," *Financial Times*, June 3, 2024, https://www.ft.com/content/d76a953d-685a-434a-8acb-36589fac2478.

4. Byron Auguste, "Low Wage, Not Low Skill: Why Devaluing Our Workers Matters," *Forbes*, February 7, 2019, https://www.forbes.com/sites/byronauguste/2019/02/07/low-wage-not-low-skill-why-devaluing-our-workers-matters/.

5. Peter Q. Blair, Tomas G. Castagnino, Erica L. Groshen, Papia Debroy, Byron Auguste, Shad Ahmed, Fernando Garcia Diaz, and Cristian Bonavida, "Searching for STARs: Work Experience as a Job Market Signal for Workers without Bachelor's Degrees," Working Paper 26844, National Bureau of Economic Research, 2020, https://www.nber.org/system/files/working_papers/w26844/w26844.pdf.

6. Blair et al., "Searching for STARs."

7. Joseph B. Fuller and Manjari Raman, *Dismissed by Degrees: How Degree Inflation is Undermining U.S. Competitiveness and Hurting America's Middle Class*, Accenture, Grads of Life, and Harvard Business School, October 2017,

https://www.hbs.edu/managing-the-future-of-work/Documents/dismissed-by-degrees.pdf.

8. Saadia Zahidi, "We Need a Global Reskilling Revolution—Here's Why," World Economic Forum, January 20, 2020, https://www.weforum.org/agenda/2020/01/reskilling-revolution-jobs-future-skills/.

9. Deloitte, *Leading the Social Enterprise: Reinvent with a Human Focus—2019 Global Human Capital Trends*, 2019, https://www2.deloitte.com/content/dam/insights/us/articles/5136_HC-Trends-2019/DI_HC-Trends-2019.pdf, pp. 85–86.

10. Tina Delligatti, Director of Human Resources, Jergens Inc., interview by Angela Jackson, March 20, 2024.

11. "Joy Buolamwini: How Do Biased Algorithms Damage Marginalized Communities?," *NPR*, October 30, 2020, https://www.npr.org/transcripts/929204946.

12. Bryan Hancock and Bill Schaninger, "Talent at a Turning Point: How People Analytics Can Help," McKinsey & Company, February 24, 2022, https://www.mckinsey.com/capabilities/people-and-organizational-performance/our-insights/talent-at-a-turning-point-how-people-analytics-can-help.

13. "2024 Global Human Capital Trends," Deloitte Insights, June 2024, https://www2.deloitte.com/us/en/insights/focus/human-capital-trends.html.

14. Ellyn Shook and Paul Daugherty, *Work, Workforce, Workers: Reinvented in the Age of Generative AI*, Accenture, January 16, 2024, https://www.accenture.com/content/dam/accenture/final/accenture-com/document-2/Accenture-Work-Can-Become-Era-Generative-AI.pdf#zoom=40.

15. Myra Norton, CEO of Arena Analytics, interview by Angela Jackson, March 29, 2023. Research by Accenture found that workforce analytics platforms can help organizations optimize their workforce planning by identifying skill gaps and providing insights into employee potential.

Chapter 7

1. Katie Sievers, interview by Angela Jackson, February 2, 2024.

2. Xperts Worker Advisory Meeting, April 26, 2021. Names have been anonymized.

3. J. R. Keller, "The Best Way to Hire from inside Your Company," *Harvard Business Review*, April 15, 2024, https://hbr.org/2015/06/the-best-way-to-hire-from-inside-your-company.

4. Jim Harter, "In New Workplace, U.S. Employee Engagement Stagnates," Gallup.com, January 23, 2024, https://www.gallup.com/workplace/608675/new-workplace-employee-engagement-stagnates.aspx.

5. Shaun Smith, Group Senior Vice President and Chief People & Culture Officer, New York Presbyterian, interview by Angela Jackson, June 7, 2024. I also interviewed him on April 12, 2023.

6. Feixia Wu, Yuewen Lao, Ying Feng, Jiaqing Zhu, Yating Zhang, and Liuyan Li, "Worldwide Prevalence and Associated Factors of Nursing Staff Turnover: A Systematic Review and Meta-Analysis," *Nursing Open* 11, no. 1 (January 2024): e2097, https://www.ncbi.nlm.nih.gov/pmc/articles/PMC10802134/.

7. Smith interview, April 12, 2023.

8. Smith interview, April 12, 2023.
9. Martin Ritter, CEO of US Stadler Rail, interview with Angela Jackson, October 4, 2023.
10. Schott, Bryan. "CEO Success Stories with Stadler US CEO Martin Ritter," Utah Policy, May 4, 2021. https://utahpolicy.com/archive/22460-ceo-success -stories-with-stadler-us-ceo-martin-ritter.
11. "Ohio Workforce Fact Sheet," Intel, September 24, 2023, https://download .intel.com/newsroom/2023/corporate/OH-Workforce-fact-sheet.pdf.
12. "Intel Invests in Ohio," Intel, March 17, 2022, https://www.intel.com /content/www/us/en/newsroom/resources/intel-invests-ohio.html#gs.cjhnx3.
13. "Diversity + Inclusion Best Practices Case Study," Manufacturing Institute, accessed July 20, 2024, https://www.themanufacturinginstitute.org/wp-content /uploads/2021/07/DI-Case-Study_Intel.pdf.
14. "Intel Corp," JUST Capital, accessed July 31, 2024, https://justcapital.com /companies/intel-corp.
15. Smith interview, June 7, 2024.
16. Smith interview, June 7, 2024.
17. Smith interview, June 7, 2024.

Chapter 8

1. Emily Bonta, Catrina Catrina Notari, Alison Omens, Aleksandra Radeva, Ian Sanders, and Kavya Vaghul, "The Current State of Human Capital Disclosure in Corporate America: Assessing What Data Large U.S. Employers Share," JUST Capital, October 5, 2021, https://justcapital.com/reports/the-current -state-of-human-capital-disclosure-in-corporate-america/.
2. US Securities and Exchange Commission, "SEC Adopts Rule Amendments to Modernize Disclosures of Business, Legal Proceedings, and Risk Factors under Regulation S-K," press release, August 8, 2020, https://www.sec.gov /newsroom/press-releases/2020-192.
3. Michael Titera and Meghan Sherley, *Evolving Human Capital Disclosures*, Gibson Dunn, January 9, 2023, https://www.gibsondunn.com/wp-content/uploads /2023/01/evolving-human-capital-disclosures.pdf.
4. Natasha Lamb, Cofounder, Managing Partner, and Portfolio Manager at Arjuna Capital, interview by Angela Jackson, February 18, 2023.
5. Lamb interview.
6. Joel Gascoigne, "Introducing Our Open Salary System: Reflecting on a Decade of Transparent Salaries at Buffer," Buffer, January 26, 2024, https:// buffer.com/resources/salary-system/.
7. Ekow Sanni-Thomas, interview by Angela Jackson, July 31, 2023.
8. Edelman Trust Institute, *2023 Edelman Trust Barometer: Global Report*, 2023, https://www.edelman.com/sites/g/files/aatuss191/files/2023-03/2023%20 Edelman%20Trust%20Barometer%20Global%20Report%20FINAL.pdf.
9. Gascoigne, "Introducing."
10. For more information, see the websites of Inside Voices (https://www .insidevoices.io/) and Glassdoor (https://www.glassdoor.com/index.htm).
11. US Securities and Exchange Commission, "SEC Adopts Rule."

Chapter 9

1. André de Waal, Michael Weaver, Tammy Day, Beatrice van der Heijden, "Silo-Busting: Overcoming the Greatest Threat to Organizational Performance," *Sustainability* 11, no. 23 (2019): 6860.

2. Howard Youngs, "Distributed Leadership," in *Oxford Research Encyclopedia of Education*, May 29, 2020, accessed July 29, 2024, https://oxfordre.com/education/view/10.1093/acrefore/9780190264093.001.0001/acrefore-9780190264093-e-612.

3. Youngs, "Distributed Leadership."

4. Youngs, "Distributed Leadership."

5. Meredith Somers, "The 3 Leadership Types in a Nimble Organization," MIT Sloan School of Management, November 1, 2021, https://mitsloan.mit.edu/ideas-made-to-matter/3-leadership-types-a-nimble-organization.

6. Somers, "3 Leadership Types."

7. Somers, "3 Leadership Types."

8. Kerry Siggins, interview by Angela Jackson, February 21, 2023.

9. "Workplace Burnout Survey: Burnout without Borders," Deloitte, April 24, 2020, https://www2.deloitte.com/us/en/pages/about-deloitte/articles/burnout-survey.html.

10. Matt Gonzales, "Here's How Bad Burnout Has Become at Work," SHRM, May 1, 2024, https://www.shrm.org/topics-tools/news/inclusion-diversity/burnout-shrm-research-2024.

11. Jenny Odell, *How to Do Nothing: Resisting the Attention Economy* (New York: Melville House, 2019); Simone Stolzoff, *The Good Enough Job: Reclaiming Life from Work* (New York: Portfolio, 2023); Oliver Burkeman, *Four Thousand Weeks: Time Management for Mortals* (New York: Vintage, 2021).

12. "Employee Ownership by the Numbers," National Center for Employee Ownership, February 2024, https://www.nceo.org/articles/employee-ownership-by-the-numbers#2.

13. Ernest H. O'Boyle, Pankaj C. Patel, and Erik Gonzalez-Mulé, "Employee Ownership and Firm Performance: A Meta-Analysis," Human Resource Management Journal 26, no. 4 (June 2016): 1–2, https://www.researchgate.net/publication/304459942_Employee_ownership_and_firm_performance_a_meta-analysis_Employee_ownership_a_meta-analysis.

14. Gallup, "The Benefits of Employee Engagement," updated January 7, 2023, accessed September 10, 2024, https://www.gallup.com/workplace/236441/benefits-employee-engagement.aspx.

15. Douglas L. Kruse, Richard B. Freeman, and Joseph R. Blasi, "Do Workers Gain by Sharing? Employee Outcomes under Employee Ownership, Profit Sharing, and Broad-Based Stock Options," in *Shared Capitalism at Work: Employee Ownership, Profit and Gain Sharing, and Broad-Based Stock Options*, ed. Douglas L. Kruse, Richard B. Freeman, and Joseph R. Blasi (Chicago: University of Chicago Press, 2010), 266; Nancy Wiefek and Nathan Nicholson, *S Corporation ESOPs and Retirement Security*, National Center for Employee Ownership, December 2018, https://www.nceo.org/assets/pdf/articles/NCEO-S-ESOPs-Retirement-Dec-2018.pdf.

16. Kruse, Freeman, and Blasi, "Do Workers Gain by Sharing?," 266.

17. Fidan Ana Kurtulus and Douglas L. Kruse, *How Did Employee Ownership Firms Weather the Last Two Recessions?: Employee Ownership, Employment Stability, and Firm Survival in the United States: 1999–2011* (Kalamazoo, MI: W. E. Upjohn Institute for Employment Research, 2017).

18. WPI Economics, *Exploring the Potential of the Employee Ownership: A Deep Dive into the Economic, People, Societal and Environmental Benefits*, October 19, 2023, https://www.efesonline.org/LIBRARY/2023/UK%20Employee%20Owner ship%20Knowledge%20Programme%202023%20-%20Detailed%20Report .pdf.

19. Kerry Siggins, interview by Angela Jackson, May 18, 2023.

Chapter 10

1. Marcus Felder, interview by Angela Jackson, July 2024.

Acknowledgments

My deepest appreciation to Steve Piersanti, Jeveen Sivasubrama-
niam, and Christy Kirk, and the entire Berrett Koehler community whose faith in me as a first-time author made this book
possible.

My thanks to my agent Mackenzie Brady Watson, who believed
in me from day one and continues to be the wind beneath my lit-
erary aspirations.

To all the individuals and companies that I interviewed for the
featured case studies in the book, I want to thank you for trust,
support, and the great work that you are doing to invest in employee thriving and Win-Win workplaces throughout the world.

As they say, no one accomplishes anything alone. I have found
this to be true in my life in general and especially true in relation
to this book. I would like to thank my personal "dream team",
Mathew Presser, Alex Amouyel, Susan McPherson, and May Jee
Bascones.

And to the women's groups that I belong to, Alpha Kappa Alpha Sorority, Chief, Extraordinary Women on Boards, and The
List, thank you for the sisterhood and for holding space to help
women meet their wildest dreams!

And to my author and publishing friends who have provided
countless hours of help and advice, Kathryn Finney, Morra

Aarons-Mele, Michael Horn, Lisen Stromberg, Laura Gassner Otting, Christina Wallace, Julia Pimsleur, Amy Webb Tabia Yapp, and Gorrik Ng.

To my forever New York City family, Deena Boykin, Diane Clear, Kevin Adams, and Neil Totton.

And to my family, Shequetta Carr, Artrell and Myra Lassiter, Jordan Lassiter, Melvin Lassiter, Leon Coe, Charles and Ranee Wilson, Iren and Ralph Sprott, Claire and John Ternan, Kyla Wells, RèMale James, Robin Delacruz, Vickie Braden, Desaree Wilcox, and Gaëlle Charlec-Jean: your unconditional love and support enable me to shoot for the stars because I know that I'll always have a soft place to land.

To Chris and Yuki, my loves. Thank you for loving me so well. And I am so very grateful for you each and every day.

Dr. Reverend Michael Beckwith inspires me weekly. He first introduced me to Howard Thurman, the author and spiritual adviser who said,

Don't ask what the world needs.
Ask what makes you come alive and go do it.
Because what the world needs is people who have come alive.

Thurman's words guide me every day. May they encourage you on your pathway to creating a Win-Win workplace!

Index

Note: Page numbers followed by n indicate notes; bold page ranges indicate primary discussion of topic.

Abbott Laboratories, 38

absenteeism, 11, 58–59, 77, 171, 178

Accenture, 107, 115, 218n15

accountability, 13, 89, 139, 146, 149, 158–159

AI. *See* artificial intelligence

Algorithmic Justice Leagues, 114

American Airlines, 2

American Opportunity Index, 15, 50

Anne E. Casey Foundation, 6

Apple, 190

apprenticeships, 128, 129–131, 141

Arena Analytics, 116–118, 129

Arjuna Capital, 142–143

artificial intelligence (AI): centering employee voices metrics with, 178; frontline leader metrics analysis with, 92, 94, 100; hiring decisions informed by, 114–115, 117–118; people analytics and, 23; skills adapted for workplace with, 110–111, 114; talent identification and development via, 106, 114–116

assets: benefits package increasing, 72, 78; centering employee voices increasing, 11, 22; distributed leadership affecting, 15, 164; frontline leaders boosting, 13; human-capital reporting increasing, 14; intersectional inclusion strengthening, 12, 64; skills-based hiring vs. credentials increasing, 13; stock ownership plans increasing, 16; talent development improving, 14, 132; Win-Win relationships increasing, 12, 38

authenticity, 12, 33–35, 59–62, 67, 144–145, 148

baby boomer generation, 33, 163

BBC, 34

benefits package, **12–13**, **19**, **69–81**;
actions to reimagine, 78–80;
brainstorming innovative, 79;
case studies of, 70–71, 72–77;
centering employee voices on, 30,
69, 74, 78–79; communication
on, 80; education and training in,
6, 71, 73, 128, 132, 134–135;
evaluation of, 74, 79–80; financial
metrics for, 16, 71–72, 77, 78;
human-capital reporting on, 76,
137–138, 140; intersectional
inclusion and, 12, 69; metrics on,
178 (*see also* financial metrics *this
entry*); personalization and flexibility of, 12, 69–70, 71, 73,
80–81; questions on, 201, 207;
refinement and adjustment of,
79–80; research findings on, 78;
ROI for, 77; significance of reimagining, 12–13, 80–81; talent
development supported by, 128,
132, 134–135; transportation in,
74–77, 79; Win-Win relationships
with, 38, 41–42, 49, 79
Ben & Jerry's, 40–44, 48–49
bias, unconscious, 65, 90, 107–109,
114, 116–118, 119
Blackstone, 172–177
Blockbuster, 190
Bock, Lazlo, 157
Bosch, 44–45
Boston Consulting Group, 94
Braden, Vickie, 70–71, 80
Branson, Richard, 62–63
bridge builders, frontline leaders as,
90

Brooks, David, 82
Buck, Sebastian, 36
Buffer, 143–145, 148
Buolamwini, Joy, 114
Burning Glass Institute, 15
burnout, 47, 54, 82, 96, 161, 163

caregivers: benefits package for, 16,
70–71, 72–73, 78, 79, 132;
hidden struggles of, 9, 55–56;
human-capital reporting on,
141–142; Win-Win relationships
and, 32–33
car trouble. *See* transportation issues
case studies, by name: Arena Analytics, 116–118; Ben & Jerry's, 40–44;
Blackstone, 172–177; Buffer,
143–145; Ekow Sanni-Thomas,
145–147; Gerald Singer, 54–55;
Jergens, Inc., 112–113; Jobina
Gonsalves, 44–45; Katie Sievers,
122–124, 125; Kerry Siggins,
160–163; Kohlberg Kravis Roberts & Co. Inc., 23–28; Morning
Star, 158–160; Natasha Lamb,
142–143; Rachel Romer, 72–74;
research methodology for, 16–17;
Shaun Smith, 127–129; Stadler
US, 129–131; Tesco and Zeelo,
74–77; Vickie Braden, 70–71;
Yamini Rangan, 59–62. *See also
under above names*
case studies, by topic: benefits package, 70–71, 72–77; centering
employee voices, 23–28; distributed leadership and entrepreneurship, 158–163; human-capital

reporting, 142–147; intersectional inclusion, 54–55, 59–62; research methodology for, 16–17; return on investment, 172–177; skills development vs. credentials, 112–113, 116–118; talent development, 122–124, 125, 127–131; Win-Win relationships, 40–45

Catalyte, 104–107

centering employee voices, **11, 18, 21–31**; actions to implement, 17, 22–23, 28–31; benefits of, 11, 16, 21, 22–23; on benefits package, 30, 69, 74, 78–79; case study of, 23–28; communication and learning with, 25, 27, 29–30; developing initiatives and programs from, 29; distributed leadership and, 30, 155, 162, 166–167; evaluation of outcomes including, 29; frontline leaders and, 92, 100; in human-capital reporting, 149–150; identifying opportunities for, 28, 63, 78–79, 100, 118, 133, 149–150, 166–167; intersectional inclusion by, 63; lack of effective, 21–22; metrics for, 178; prioritization of, 28–29; questions on, 199, 206; refinement of changes by, 29; research findings on, 22; on skills, 118; social justice with, 41; strategies to embrace, 30–31; talent development by, 133; Win-Win relationships built by, 30, 47–48

CEO Jobs Council, 135–136

Chamber of Commerce, 9

Chartered Management Institute, 85

ChatGPT, 110

Chevron, 107

childcare: in benefits package, 16, 71, 72–73, 78, 79, 132; company on-site, 73, 79; hidden struggles with, 9, 55–56; human-capital reporting on, 141–142; Win-Win relationships and, 32–33

China, work environments in, 34

C.H.I. Overhead Doors, 24–28, 29, 30, 150

Chrysler Motors, 3–4, 190

City University of New York, 136

class, social. *See* socioeconomic status

Cognizant, 107

collaboration: benefits package effects on, 73; centering employee voices with, 29; core collaboration hours for, 97; distributed leadership increasing, 14, 155, 158–160; frontline leaders fostering, 95, 97, 98; human-AI, 111; human-capital reporting encouraging, 144–145, 148, 152; intersectional inclusion fostering, 67; ROI and, 171, 174; on skills-based hiring, 119; talent development enhancing, 124; Win-Win relationships fostering, 12, 40, 48, 178

Colleague Letter of Understanding, 158–159

communication: on benefits package, 80; centering employee voices and, 25, 27, 29–30; distributed leadership fostering, 155, 160, 168–169; with frontline leaders, 96, 98, 102; on human-capital

communication (*continued*)
reporting, 151–152, 179; intersectional inclusion fostering, 65, 66–67; on rewards of Win-Win workplace, 195–196; on ROI, 175–176, 182, 185–186; on skills-based hiring, 120; on talent development, 135–136; transparency of (*see* transparency); on Win-Win pillar implementation, 18; Win-Win relationships built on, 43, 46, 49

compensation. *See* benefits package; wages

continuous improvement, 80, 92, 99, 175–176, 187–188, 195

Corporate Snark, 34

costs: benefits package and, 71, 73, 76, 77, 79; centering employee voices reducing, 27–28, 30; of credential mandates, 108; of education and training, 43, 47, 110; of hidden identities, 54–55; of hiring, 108–109, 175, 176; metrics on, 180 (*see also* ROI *this entry*); of presenteeism, 58–59; of recruitment, 43, 47, 77; in ROI, 180, 181, 182; self-management saving, 159; sunk, 181; of talent development lack, 126–127; of transportation, 57–58, 76–77; of turnover, 12, 36, 39–40, 175, 176

Covey, Stephen, 97

COVID-19 pandemic: Great Resignation with, 37; human-capital reporting on, 138; purpose and meaning of work reevaluated in, 163; transportation in, 75; workplace shifts due to, 1, 4–5, 10, 189

credentials, **13**, **19–20**, **104–121**; actions to implement alternatives to, 118–120; bias for, eliminating, 107–109, 116–118, 119; case study of alternatives to, 112–113, 116–118; competencies vs., 109–110; limitations of, 104–106, 108; metrics on skills-based hiring vs., 119, 179; questions on, 202–203, 207; refinement and adjustment of alternatives to, 119–120; rethinking traditional, 105–106, 121; STARS or skills vs., 13, 105–121, 179; talent development regardless of, 127–128, 131, 132; technology assisting alternatives to, 106, 110–111, 113–116

Crenshaw, Kimberlé, 53

customer loyalty and satisfaction: centering employee voices increasing, 23; frontline leaders' effect on, 90–91, 93; human-capital reporting effects on, 138–139, 144, 148, 151; metrics on, 171, 180; Net Promoter Score of, 21; ROI and, 171; Win-Win relationships increasing, 38, 39, 41; Zero-Sum workplace reducing, 11

Cuyahoga East Vocational Education Consortium, 113

data analysis: bias elimination via, 116–118; on centering employee voices, 178; of frontline leader metrics, 92–94, 96, 100, 101; human-capital reporting using (*see* human-capital reporting); of intersectional inclusion metrics, 62–63, 66; of New Profit Future of Work Grand Challenge applicants, 8–10; people analytics and, 21, 23; predictive, 115; of ROI, 181, 184–185; of skills, 109, 110, 114–118; of talent development programs, 134; for talent identification and development, 114–116; Win-Win relationship refinement using, 49. *See also* metrics; research; surveys

debt, 38, 57, 79

decision-making: centering employee voices in, 21, 26, 133, 167; data-driven, 14, 91, 149, 187; with distributed leadership, 14, 156–157, 158–159, 166, 169, 179; frontline leaders and, 13, 91, 95; human-capital reporting informing, 14; ROI informing, 185–186

Dell, 95–96, 102

Deloitte, 111, 115, 147, 163

dependent care. *See* caregivers; childcare

disabilities, persons with, 52, 53, 55–56, 113

distributed leadership, **14–15**, **20**, **153–169**; actions to implement, 166–169; case studies of, 158–163;

centering employee voices in, 30, 155, 162, 166–167; communication with, 155, 160, 168–169; definition of, 154; entrepreneurship for, 14–15, 30, 153–169, 179, 204, 208; evaluation of, 168; innovation increased with, 14, 154–156, 158–159, 162, 168, 169, 179; metrics on, 168, 179; nimble organizations with, 156–158; ownership and, 14, 132, 153–154, 158–159, 160–163, 164–166, 169; purpose and meaning of work with, 163–164, 166; questions on, 204, 208; refinement and adjustment of, 168; research findings on, 164–166; self-management and, 158–160, 167

diversity: credentials vs. skills and, 13, 105, 108, 109, 119, 121; frontline leaders celebrating, 89; human-capital reporting on, 137–138, 140, 145–147; intersectional inclusion and, 52–53, 59, 61–64, 67, 89; as return on investment, 177; talent development increasing, 129, 133–134; Win-Win relationships embracing, 42–43, 44–45

Drucker, Peter, 46

EAPs (Employee Assistance Programs), 140

Edelman Trust Barometer, 148

education and training: apprenticeships as, 128, 129–131, 141; in
benefits package, 6, 71, 73, 128,
132, 134–135; credentials from
(*see* credentials); for distributed
leadership, 160, 167; for frontline
leaders, 82, 87, 92–95, 98–103,
178; human-capital reporting on,
14, 137, 140–141; in intersectional inclusion initiatives, 65;
skills-based hiring reducing costs
of, 110; skills development with,
112–113; student loan debt
assistance for, 38, 79; talent
development and, 14, 128,
129–131, 132, 134–136, 179;
tuition assistance for, 128, 132,
134–135; Win-Win People Leader
Training as, 98–99; Win-Win
relationships reducing costs of, 43,
47
efficiency: AI and data analysis
improving, 114–115; benefits
package improving, 80; centering
employee voices for, 23; distributed leadership enabling, 154,
158–159; frontline leaders and,
91; human-capital reporting
improving, 144, 148; intersectional inclusion leveraging,
54; as return on investment,
171; talent development
enhancing, 124, 129; Win-Win
relationships including, 36,
38
Employee Assistance Programs
(EAPs), 140

Employee Ownership Association,
166
employee resource groups (ERGs),
66
employees: benefits for (*see* benefits
package); centering voices of (*see*
centering employee voices); credentials of (*see* credentials); empowerment of (*see* empowerment);
engagement of (*see* engagement);
entrepreneurship among (*see* entrepreneurship); human-capital
reporting on (*see* human-capital
reporting); intersectional inclusion
of (*see* intersectional inclusion);
leadership by (*see* leadership);
longevity of (*see* retention; turnover); personal lives of (*see* personal lives); recruitment and
hiring of (*see* hiring; recruitment); ROI communicated to,
186; talent of (*see* skills; talent);
Win-Win relationships with
(*see* Win-Win relationships); Win-
Win workplace with (*see* Win-Win
workplace)
Employee Stock Ownership Plans
(ESOPs), 16, 42, 49, 132,
162–163, 164–165. *See also*
stock ownership
empowerment: apprenticeships for,
131; discussion guide as tool for,
197–198; with distributed leadership, 14, 20, 153–159, 167, 169;
by frontline leaders, 98, 102; of
frontline leaders, 13, 82, 87,
91–93, 99; human-capital

reporting increasing, 144, 147,
148; intersectional inclusion for,
59; metrics and ROI supporting,
176–177, 188; as reward of
Win-Win workplace, 5, 190;
skills development for, 111;
Win-Win relationships fostering,
45, 46, 50

Empower Work, 87

engagement: on benefits package,
79; centering employee voices
fostering, 23, 24–25, 27–28, 178;
credentials and, 108; definition of,
39; distributed leadership increasing, 157, 165, 168; frontline
leaders and, 13, 88, 90, 91–93,
101, 178; human-capital reporting improving, 147, 150–151;
intersectional inclusion increasing,
63, 64, 65–66, 68; metrics on,
179 (*see also* ROI *this entry*);
ROI and, 177, 186; talent
development and, 123, 124,
126, 134; in transactional relationships, 39; in Win-Win relationships, 38, 39, 41, 46, 48–49,
178

enslaved people, 35

Enso Future Design, 36

entrepreneurship, **14–15, 153–169**;
actions to implement, 166–169;
case studies of, 158–163; centering employee voices for, 30, 155,
162, 166–167; communication
with, 155, 160, 168–169; distributed leadership via, 14–15,
30, 153–169, 179, 204, 208;
innovation increased with, 14,
154–156, 158–159, 162, 168,
169, 179; nimble organizations
with, 156–158; ownership and,
14, 153–154, 158–159, 160–163,
164–166, 169; purpose and
meaning of work with, 163–164,
166; questions on, 204, 208;
refinement and adjustment
of, 168; research findings on,
164–166; self-management and,
158–160, 167; structure supporting, 30, 154, 157–158, 164,
166–169

environmental, social, and
governance (ESG) practices/
environmental issues, 77, 139,
143

ERGs (employee resource groups),
66

ESOPs. *See* Employee Stock Ownership Plans

ethical practices, 64, 111, 114

ethnicity. *See* race and ethnicity

evaluation: of benefits package, 74,
79–80; centering employee voices
in, 29; of distributed leadership,
168; of frontline leader programs,
101; of human-capital reporting,
151; of intersectional inclusion,
66; performance, 21, 92, 100,
109, 178; of skills, 13, 109, 118;
of skills-based hiring, 119; of
talent development programs,
134–135; of Win-Win pillar
implementation, 18; Win-Win
relationship methods of, 49

facilitator guide, **205–209**

Fairtrade certification, 42

feedback, employee. *See* centering employee voices

Feeding America, 56

Felder, Marcus, 172–177

financial metrics. *See* assets; costs; profits; return on investment; revenue; valuation

flexible teams, 111

flexible work arrangements: benefits package including, 71, 79; frontline leaders and, 96, 97; human-capital reporting on, 143; intersectional inclusion and, 61, 65, 67

FlexJobs, 34

Floyd, George, 146

focus groups, 49, 63, 66, 118, 133, 166, 179

focus time, 97

food insecurity, 56

Four Seasons, 2

France, work environments in, 34

frontline leaders, **13, 19, 82–103**; actions to develop strong, 13, 93–97, 100–102; author's experience as, 83–85; becoming Win-Win leaders, 97–99, 102–103; centering employee voices on, 92, 100; challenges of, 82–83, 87, 94; core competencies of, 100; customer experience affected by, 90–91, 93; data analysis of, 92–94, 96, 100, 101; empowerment of, 13, 82, 87, 91–93, 99; evaluation of programs for, 101; flexible

work arrangements and focus time for, 96, 97; Global People Leaders as, 90–94; high-, medium-, and low-performing, 93; incentives for, 88; intersectional inclusion boosted by, 13, 83, 87, 89–90, 99; listening and communication with, 96, 98, 102; management training for, 82, 87, 92–95, 98–103, 178; metrics on, 91–94, 100, 101, 178; onboarding of, 100–101; ownership mindset fostered by, 13, 87, 89; promotion to, 83–85, 98, 100; questions on, 202, 207; refinement and adjustment of programs for, 101–102; research findings on, 99; roles of, 82, 95, 102–103; support resources for, 87–88, 96, 103; values championed by, 87, 88–89, 103; Win-Win value of supporting, 85–87

Future Forum, 94

Future Forward Strategies, 11, 98

Gallup polls, 22, 23, 28, 37, 39, 91, 126

Gascoigne, Joel, 145

Gelsinger, Patrick, 132

gender: frontline leaders and, 86–87; intersectional inclusion by, 53, 63, 64; parenthood, leadership, and, 72–73; pay gaps by, 143, 149

Gen X, 33, 163–164

Gen Z, 33, 56, 164

Gibson Dunn, 137–138

Glassdoor, 15, 150

Gleeson Recruitment Group, 34
Global People Leaders, 17, 90–94
Gonsalves, Jobina, 44–45, 46
Google, 107, 147, 157
Grads of Life, 172–174
Great Resignation, 36–37
Greenfield, Jerry, 41
Guild Education, 72–73, 74, 78,
    79, 80

Halligan, Brian, 60
Harvard Business Review, 62, 82,
    126, 148
Hayes, Vanice, 96
health issues: benefits package and,
    70–71, 79; hidden struggles with,
    56; human-capital reporting on,
    137, 140; presenteeism and,
    58–59; workplace environment
    effect on, 40, 47, 161. *See also*
    mental health issues
health system, 116–118, 127–129,
    133–135
H-E-B, 95, 102
Hewitt, Olivia, 173, 175
hierarchies. *See under* organizational
    structure
hiring: AI informing, 114–115,
    117–118; costs of, 108–109,
    175, 176; credentials in (*see* cre-
    dentials); external employees vs.
    internal talent, 122, 124, 127;
    human-capital reporting on,
    140–142; skills and talent
    as criteria for, 13, 105–121,
    174–175, 179; Zero-Sum, 124.
    See also recruitment

Holmes, Michael, 76–77
home-based work. *See* remote
    work
housing issues, 56, 58, 74, 79
HubSpot, 59, 60–62, 67
human-capital reporting, **14, 20,
    137–152**; actions to implement,
    149–152; benefits package in, 76,
    137–138, 140; case studies on,
    142–147; centering employee
    voices in, 149–150; communica-
    tion on, 151–152, 179; as com-
    petitive strategy, 14, 139, 142,
    144–145, 148–152; data points
    and metrics in, 14, 139, 140–141,
    150, 179; diversity and DEI
    initiatives in, 137–138, 140,
    145–147; evaluation of, 151;
    intersectional inclusion and,
    139, 147; questions to inform,
    141–142, 203–204, 208; refine-
    ment and adjustment of, 150–151;
    requirements for, 137, 151; re-
    search findings on, 149; status of,
    137–138; transparency and radi-
    cal openness in, 14, 137–139,
    142–145, 148–149, 150–152;
    Win-Win workplace approach to,
    139–142
human connection, culture of. *See*
    Win-Win relationships

identities, intersectional. *See*
    intersectional inclusion
imposter syndrome, 60–61
incentives, for frontline leaders, 88
initiative takers, 89

innovation: centering employee voices for, 23; commitment to, 195; distributed leadership increasing, 14, 154–156, 158–159, 162, 168, 169, 179; human-capital reporting encouraging, 144, 147, 148; intersectional inclusion fostering, 62, 64, 67; as return on investment, 171, 177; skills-based hiring improving, 121; talent development and, 124, 126; Win-Win relationships fostering, 40, 43, 45, 50

Inside Voices, 146–147, 149–150

Intel, 131–132, 151

Intermountain Healthcare, 135

internal promotions. *See* talent development

International Labor Organization, 56

internships, 128

intersectional inclusion, **12**, **19**, **52–68**; actions to create, 53–54, 63, 65–67; authenticity fostered by, 12, 59–62, 67; benefits of, 12, 52–54, 64, 67–68; benefits package and, 12, 69; case studies of, 54–55, 59–62; centering employee voices for, 63; communication fostered with/on, 65, 66–67; credentials and, 105; definition of, 53; economic returns with, 62–63, 64, 176–177; evaluation of, 66; frontline leaders boosting, 13, 83, 87, 89–90, 99; hidden struggles and, 54–56; human-capital reporting and, 139, 147; metrics on, 178 (*see also* economic returns *this entry*); power of, 59; questions on, 200–201, 206–207; refinement and adjustment of, 65–67; research findings on, 64; ROI and, 176–177; strategies for implementing, 65–66; strengths-based, 65–66; talent development and, 133–134; understanding employee challenges for, 56–59; unlocking potential with, 62–63

investors, 7, 138–139, 186. *See also* stock ownership

Janzer, Christina, 96–97

Jergens, Inc., 4, 112–113

Jobcase, 107

job descriptions, 110, 115–116, 118, 134

Journal of Applied Psychology, 57

Journal of Business and Psychology, 57

Joyce Foundation, 6

JPMorgan Chase, 9

JUST Capital, 15, 38, 132, 137

Kanarys, 146–147

Kenya, work environments in, 34

key performance indicators (KPIs), 168, 181

Kimpton Hotel & Restaurant Group, 38

Kohlberg Kravis Roberts & Co. Inc. (KKR), 23–28, 29, 30–31

Lamb, Natasha, 142–143

layoffs, 7, 123, 125, 165

leadership: distributed (*see* distributed leadership); frontline (*see* frontline leaders); parenthood and, 72–73; ROI communicated to, 186; talent development toward, 13, 133, 134–136; transparency modeled by, 151–152; Win-Win, 97–99, 102–103, 190–192

legal compliance, 64, 137, 151

LinkedIn, 15, 107

linked prosperity, 41–44, 49

listening, 96. *See also* centering employee voices

Living Wage Percentage (LWP), 38–39, 141–142

loyalty: benefits package heightening, 13, 73; customer (*see* customer loyalty and satisfaction); frontline leaders building, 86; human-capital reporting increasing, 138; as return on investment, 171, 177; talent development fostering, 132, 135; in transactional relationships, 37, 39; Win-Win relationships building, 39, 47

machine learning, 94, 100, 106, 114, 115, 116, 178

Management Leadership for Tomorrow, 94

Mandarin Oriental, 2

market relevance, 43, 68

maternity leave, 71–72, 78, 79, 80

Mayer, Marissa, 72–73

McDonald's, 9

McKinsey & Company, 62, 107, 114–115, 148

mental health issues: benefits package on, 79; frontline leaders and, 96, 101; hidden struggles with, 56, 57; human-capital reporting on, 140; presenteeism and, 58–59; Win-Win relationships supporting, 38; workplace environment effect on, 40, 57, 161. *See also* psychological safety

mentoring, 65, 93, 98, 131, 133, 140, 154

metrics, **20**, **170–188**; on benefits package, 178; for centering employee voices, 178; common Win-Win, 179–180; continuous improvement with, 175–176, 187–188; on cost savings, 180; on customer satisfaction, 171, 180; on distributed leadership, 168, 179; on engagement, 179; financial (*see* assets; costs; profits; return on investment; revenue; valuation); on frontline leader effectiveness, 91–94, 100, 101, 178; on human capital (*see* human-capital reporting); identifying key, 177–179; on intersectional inclusion, 178; on productivity, 171, 180 (*see also* efficiency; productivity); on retention, 180; rewards of Win-Win workplace supported by, 193; on skills-based hiring, 119, 179; for talent development, 134, 179; on Win-Win relationships, 178

Microsoft, 40

middle managers. *See* frontline leaders

Millennial generation, 33, 164

MillerKnoll, 94

mindset: entrepreneurial, 155, 160; human-capital reporting open disclosure, 138; ownership, 13, 87, 89, 154, 162, 164; Win-Win, 97–98, 102

MIT, 9

morale: employee voices not heard lowering, 25; frontline leaders and, 88, 91; intersectional inclusion improving, 63; as return on investment, 171; talent development and, 126, 129; in transactional relationships, 39; workplace environment effect on, 40

Morning Star, 158–160, 167

MTV, 190

Musk, Elon, 62–63

mutualistic working relationships. *See* Win-Win relationships

Netflix, 190

Net Promoter Score, 21

neurodiversity, 62–63, 65

New Profit, 8–11

New York–Presbyterian, 127–129, 133–135

New York Times, 58, 82

19th, The, 95

996 work culture, 34

Nokia, 2

Norton, Myra, 116

Occupational Health Science, 40

onboarding, 100–101, 126

Opportunity@Work, 106

organizational structure: command-and-control, 35; with distributed leadership and entrepreneurship, 14, 20, 30, 154–155, 157–160, 164, 166–169; hierarchies in, 6, 14, 35, 50, 58, 129, 155, 166, 169, 191; intersectional inclusion and, 58; self-management in, 158–160, 167; talent development and, 129; Win-Win leadership changing, 191–192; Win-Win relationships and, 34, 35, 50; Zero-Sum workplace, 6

ownership, employee: centering employee voices and, 25–27, 28–29; distributed leadership with culture of, 14, 132, 153–154, 158–159, 160–163, 164–166, 169; financial benefits of, 16; frontline leaders fostering mindset for, 13, 87, 89; human-capital reporting on, 141, 150; pathways to, 160–163; Win-Win relationships with, 42, 49. *See also* stock ownership

Oxford University, 154–155

paid time off, 71, 78

parenthood: benefits package and, 16, 71–73, 78, 79–80, 132; frontline leaders accommodating, 83; intersectional inclusion of, 67; leadership and, 72–73; Win-Win relationships and, 32–33. *See also* childcare

paternity leave, 16, 72, 78, 79

pay. *See* wages

people analytics, 21, 23

performance evaluations, 21, 92, 100, 109, 178

personal lives: benefits package appropriate for, 12, 69–71, 73, 80–81; intersectional inclusion of (*see* intersectional inclusion); Win-Win relationships acknowledging effects of, 32–35. *See also* caregivers; childcare; parenthood; work-life balance

Peter, Laurence J., 85

Peter Principle, 85

pillars of Win-Win workplace, **11–15, 199–204**. *See also specific pillars*

poverty rates, 141–142

presenteeism, 58–59

Prism Work, 86

problem-solving, 14, 62, 89, 121, 153, 159

productivity: benefits package improving, 77, 78, 79; centering employee voices improving, 23, 24, 26, 27–28, 30; credentials not equated with, 107, 108; distributed leadership improving, 158–159, 163, 165, 168, 179; frontline leaders' effect on, 87, 91; intersectional inclusion improving, 63, 68; metrics on, 171, 180; presenteeism effects on, 58–59; ROI and, 171; skills-based hiring improving, 110, 121; talent development lack decreasing, 126;

Win-Win relationships increasing, 38, 39, 46, 47, 50; Zero-Sum workplace reducing, 11

professional development. *See* education and training

profits: benefits package improving, 13, 16, 72, 78; centering employee voices increasing, 11, 22, 23, 28, 31; distributed leadership increasing, 15, 163, 164–165; employee profit-sharing plans with, 25; frontline leaders' effect on, 13, 91; human-capital reporting increasing, 14, 139, 149; human lives as secondary to, 35–36; intersectional inclusion increasing, 12, 62; skills-based hiring vs. credentials improving, 13; talent development improving, 16; Win-Win relationships increasing, 12, 38, 39, 50

psychological safety, 46, 98, 148, 178

race and ethnicity: diversity by (*see* diversity); human-capital reporting on issues of, 145–147, 149; intersectional inclusion by, 53, 62, 63, 64; pay gaps by, 143, 149

Rangan, Yamini, 59–62, 65–66, 67

recruitment, 43, 47, 76, 77, 126, 130, 140. *See also* hiring

reduction in force, 7. *See also* layoffs

remote work, 10, 37, 61, 70, 101, 142–143

research: on benefits package, 78; case studies from (*see* case studies, by name; case studies, by topic); on centering employee voices, 22; on distributed leadership, 164–166; on flexible teams and talent mobility, 111; on frontline leaders, 99; on human-capital reporting, 149; on intersectional inclusion, 64; on talent development, 132; on Win-Win relationships, 38–39; on Win-Win workplace, generally, 1–5, 8–11, 15–17. *See also* data analysis; surveys

resignations, 36–37, 39–40, 86, 125. *See also* turnover

respect, 40, 41, 51, 89, 109

results-oriented employees, 89

retention: benefits package effects on, 76, 77, 79; centering employee voices improving, 16, 22; credentials not equated with, 107; distributed leadership improving, 158–159; frontline leaders' effect on, 86, 92, 178; human-capital reporting on, 138, 140–142, 147; intersectional inclusion improving, 63, 64; metrics on, 180; as return on investment, 171, 177; talent development increasing, 14, 130, 132; Win-Win relationships improving, 43, 45, 47, 50

return on investment (ROI), **20**, **170–177**, **180–188**; actions for improvement based on, 184–185; actions to measure and implement, 174–176, 180–183; for benefits package, 77; calculation of, 182; case study on, 172–177; communication on, 175–176, 182, 185–186; continuous improvement with, 175–176, 187–188; costs and investments in, 180, 181, 182; defining measurable outcomes for, 181; definition and dimensions of, 170–171; financial, 171; frontline leaders' effect on, 93; identifying successful and less successful areas with, 184; interpretation and actionable insights from, 183–184; organizational, 171; projection of, 181; refining measurement of, 175–176, 181; rewards of Win-Win workplace supported by, 193; social, 171; strategy and objectives for, 180, 193; talent development and, 171, 172–177; tangible and intangible, 171, 183; timeframe for, 183; tracking and analysis of, 181, 184–185; Win-Win relationships improving, 50

revenue: benefits package increasing, 72, 78; centering employee voices increasing, 11, 16, 22, 28; distributed leadership affecting, 15, 156, 164; human-capital reporting increasing, 14, 149; ROI and, 171; stock ownership plans increasing, 16; Win-Win relationships increasing, 38, 50

rewards of Win-Win workplace, **189–196**; achievability of, 5,

194–195; acknowledgment and recognition of, 189–190; call to action to achieve, 194; communication on successful, 195–196; future steps toward, 195; metrics underpinning, 193; Win-Win leaders benefiting from, 190–192

Richards, Genevieve, 54–55, 57, 58, 95

right to disconnect legislation, 34

Ritter, Martin, 129

ROI. *See* return on investment

Romer, Rachel, 72–74, 78, 79, 80, 215n6

Rosenbaum, Mike, 104–106

Rosenblum, Elyse, 172–173

Rosenthal, Caitlin, 35–36

Rufer, Chris, 158

Ryan, Sam, 75

safety issues: centering employee voices on, 24, 27; COVID-19 pandemic and, 37; human-capital reporting on, 137–138, 140, 147; training on, 6; Win-Win relationships addressing, 45. *See also* psychological safety

Sanni-Thomas, Ekow, 145–147, 149–150

satisfaction, customer. *See* customer loyalty and satisfaction

satisfaction, employee: benefits package effects on, 13, 71, 73, 76, 79, 178; centering employee voices improving, 21, 27; distributed leadership improving, 158–159, 165–166, 179; frontline leaders'

effect on, 85–86, 91, 178; human-capital reporting on, 140–141; intersectional inclusion improving, 57, 63, 68; lack of, 22, 36; as return on investment, 171; Win-Win relationships leading to, 47

Schron, Jack, Jr., 112–113

Schron, Jack, Sr., 112

Schwab, Charles, 62–63

Sears, 190

Securities and Exchange Commission (US), 137, 151

self-management, 158–160, 167

Semiconductor Education and Research Program, 131

7 Habits of Highly Effective People, The (Covey), 97

sexuality/sexual orientation, 53

Shulman, Jeff, 7

sick leave, 71

Sievers, Katie, 122–124, 125, 126

Siggins, Kerry, 160–163, 167, 169, 191–192

Singer, Gerald, 54–55, 57

Skilled Through Alternative Routes (STARS), 13, 105–110, 113, 131–132

skills: actions to implement hiring based on, 118–120; core competencies and, 100, 109–110; credentials vs., 13, 105–121, 179; education and training to improve (*see* education and training); evaluation of, 13, 109, 118; factory closure and obsolete, 3–4; hiring for, 13, 105–121, 174–175, 179; intersectional inclusion beyond, 52;

skills (*continued*)
job descriptions on, 110, 115–116, 118; research on upskilling of, 8–10; standardized classification of, 115–116; talent optimization via, 109–111; technology effects on, 8–9, 110–111, 113–114. *See also* talent
SkyHive, 40
Slack, 9, 94, 95–97, 102, 152
slavery, 35
Smith, Shaun, 127–129, 133–136
Social & Environmental Assessment Reports, 43
social justice, 40–42
social responsibility, 64
Society for Human Resource Management, 9, 40, 163
Society of Manufacturing Engineers, 112
socioeconomic status: credentials vs. skills and, 105, 110, 118; intersectional inclusion by, 53, 57; parenthood and, 73; poverty rates and, 141–142
Sotomayor, Sonia, 32–33
Stadler US, 129–131
STARS (Skilled Through Alternative Routes), 13, 105–110, 113, 131–132
Stavros, Pete, 23–28, 29, 30
stereotyping, 57
stigma, 56, 57, 66
stock ownership: centering employee voices and, 11, 26–27; distributed leadership via, 132, 162–163, 164–166; financial benefits of

employee, 16; talent development and, 132; Win-Win relationships with, 42, 49; Zero-Sum workplace, 7. *See also* investors; ownership, employee
StoneAge, 161–163, 167, 191–192
strengths-based focus, 65–66
Stromberg, Lisen, 86–87
structure, organizational. *See* organizational structure
student loan debt assistance, 38, 79
suggestion boxes, 11, 21, 152, 167, 179
support resources, 87–88, 96, 103
surveys: on benefits package, 78–79; centering employee voices and, 21, 25, 28, 63, 78–79, 118, 133, 166, 178; on distributed leadership, 166, 168; on diversity, 146; on engagement, 179; on frontline leaders, 86–87, 92, 94–95, 96; on human-capital reporting, 151; on intersectional inclusion, 63, 66, 178; pulse, 92, 96, 178; on skills and competencies, 110, 118; for talent development, 133; Win-Win relationships using, 49, 178; on workplace environments, 34, 40. *See also* Gallup polls
Swimming with Sharks (film), 84

Taco Bell, 104
talent: developing internal pools of (*see* talent development); hiring for, 105–110, 114–115; internal mobility of, 16, 111, 125, 128–129,

134–135; management of, 115; research on, 111, 132; skills-based optimization of, 109–111; standardized classification of, 115–116; technology to identify and develop, 106, 114–116, 119, 129; workforce planning to optimize, 115, 218n15. *See also* skills

talent development, **13–14**, **20**, **122–136**; actions to implement, 124, 133–136; apprenticeships for, 128, 129–131; benefits of, 13–14, 16, 124, 129; benefits package supporting, 128, 132, 134–135; case studies on, 122–124, 125, 127–131; centering employee voices in, 133; communication on, 135–136; costs of overlooking, 126–127; credentials not determinant for, 127–128, 131, 132; deep benches of, 13–14, 124, 132–136; distributed leadership and, 166; evaluation of, 134–135; failure to cultivate, 122–124, 125–127; hiring external employees vs., 122, 124, 127; human-capital reporting on, 138, 141–142; intersectional inclusion and, 133–134; metrics for, 134, 179 (*see also* ROI *this entry*); questions on, 203, 208; refinement and adjustment of, 134–135; research findings on, 132; ROI and, 171, 172–177; STARS and, 131–132; wages and, 124, 132

talent gaps, 123

Tear the Paper Ceiling campaign, 107

technology: AI (*see* artificial intelligence); ethical issues and, 111, 114; machine learning (*see* machine learning); skills and, 8–9, 110–111, 113–114; talent identification and development via, 106, 114–116, 119, 129

Tesco, 74–77, 79, 80

Thomas, Jill, 116–117

360-degree reviews, 21, 178

Tooling U, 112–113

training. *See* education and training

Training (magazine), 99

transactional relationships, 4, 5, 35, 36–37, 39

transparency: on benefits package, 73, 74, 80; centering employee voices and, 25, 30–31; in distributed leadership, 169; in human-capital reporting, 14, 137–139, 142–145, 148–149, 150–152; in talent development, 134; on Win-Win pillar implementation, 18; in Win-Win relationships, 43

transportation issues, 9, 33, 55, 57–58, 74–77, 79

trust building: centering employee voices for, 25, 27, 149; distributed leadership for, 158, 160, 169; frontline leaders for, 86, 98; human-capital reporting for, 14, 143–145, 147, 148, 149, 150, 152; Win-Win relationships for, 40, 46, 47, 178

tuition assistance, 128, 132, 134–135

turnover: benefits package lowering, 79; centering employee voices reducing, 11, 21, 23; costs of, 12, 36, 39–40, 175, 176; credentials and, 108; distributed leadership decreasing, 159; frontline leaders' effect on, 13, 86, 91; human-capital reporting on, 138, 140–142; inequity leading to, 36; intersectional inclusion reducing, 63, 64; ROI and, 176; skills-based hiring reducing, 110, 117; talent development and, 124, 126, 129; voluntary vs. regrettable, 176; Win-Win relationships decreasing, 12, 38, 39, 47; in Zero-Sum workplace, 11
TÜV SÜD, 4, 44–45

Unilever, 49
unions, 48–49
United Airlines, 2
United Kingdom: benefits packages in, 74–77; employee ownership in, 165–166; frontline leaders in, 85; work environments in, 34
United Way, 9
Urban Institute, 56

vacation time, 71. *See also* paid time off
valuation: benefits package increasing, 13, 16, 72, 78; centering employee voices increasing, 22; distributed leadership improving, 15, 164; frontline leaders improving, 13; human-capital reporting increasing, 14; intersectional inclusion improving, 64; skills-based hiring vs. credentials increasing, 13; talent development increasing, 14, 16; Win-Win relationships increasing, 38
value chains, 23, 28
values: benefits package reflecting, 69; employee, 33, 37, 40, 44–45; frontline leaders championing, 87, 88–89, 103; human-capital reporting reflecting, 138–139, 143, 144, 148, 149; organizational culture reflecting, 43–46, 48; social justice, 40–42; Win-Win leaders embodying, 190–192
veterans, 53–55
voices, centering employee. *See* centering employee voices

wages: credentials vs. skills effects on, 108, 110; employee ownership and, 165–166; for external hires, 124; of frontline leaders, 103; human-capital reporting on, 14, 137–138, 140–143, 145, 149; Living Wage Percentage, 38–39, 141–142; pay gaps in, 143, 149; talent development and, 124, 132; in transactional relationships, 4, 37; turnover costs and, 39–40; Win-Win relationships and, 12, 38–39, 41, 50
Walmart, 4, 107, 190
Wednesday Forums, 128–129, 133
Westfall, Sandra Sobieraj, 32–33

whole person inclusion. *See* intersectional inclusion

Win-Win mindset, 97–98, 102

Win-Win People Leader Training, 98–99

Win-Win relationships, **12**, **18**, **32–51**; actions to implement, 32–33, 47–49; authenticity vs. artifice in, 33–35; benefits of, 12, 46–47; benefits package strengthening, 38, 41–42, 49, 79; building of, 50–51; case studies of, 40–45; centering employee voices creating, 30, 47–48; communication in, 43, 46, 49; connection promoted in, 34, 37, 38, 40, 41, 43, 46–49, 50, 178; employee engagement in, 38, 39, 41, 46, 48–49, 178; evaluation of outcomes in, 49; history leading to lack of, 35–36; linked prosperity with, 41–44, 49; metrics on, 178; overcoming challenges of, 50; questions on, 200, 206; refinement of, 48–49; relational company culture empowering, 46; research findings on, 38–39; resignations and, 36–37, 39–40; transactional relationships vs., 4, 5, 35, 36–37, 39

Win-Win workplace: actions to change to, 17–18, 19; conceptualization of, 11–16; definition and description of, 5, 7–8; discussion guide on, 197–198; employees in (*see* employees); facilitator guide on, 205–209; key findings on, 16; leadership in (*see* leadership); measurement of impact and ROI in (*see* metrics); pillars of, 11–15, 199–204 (*see also specific pillars*); reaping rewards of (*see* rewards of Win-Win workplace); research on, 1–5, 8–11, 15–17; toolkit for, 237–238; Win-Win relationships in (*see* Win-Win relationships); Zero-Sum workplace vs. (*see* Zero-Sum workplace)

Wolgamott, John, 161–162

Workday, 40, 107

workforce composition, 140. *See also* diversity

workforce planning, 14, 115, 218n15

work from home. *See* remote work

work-life balance: benefits package and, 71, 74; COVID-19 pandemic and, 37; frontline leaders addressing, 83; human-capital reporting on, 140, 143; purpose and meaning of work for, 164; Win-Win relationships and, 40; Zero-Sum workplace effects on, 6. *See also* personal lives

workplace: employees in (*see* employees); shifts in, 1, 4–5, 10, 189; toxic, 34, 84; Win-Win (*see* Win-Win workplace); Zero-Sum (*see* Zero-Sum workplace)

World Economic Forum, 111

World Health Organization, 56

Yahoo!, 72

Zeelo, 75–77, 81

Zero-Sum workplace: benefits package in, 69, 71; credentials in, 105; definition of, 6; employee engagement in, 39; employee voices not heard in, 22, 26; failures of, 6–8, 11; frontline leaders in, 87; hiring practices in, 124; human-capital reporting lack in, 138, 146, 150; intersectional inclusion omitted in, 52; leadership in, 87, 155, 160–161, 169; risks of maintaining, 189–190; ROI in, 171; talent development lack in, 124, 126; Win-Win relationships vs., 35, 47; Win-Win workplace vs., 7–8, 11

Zink, Jerry, 161–162

The Win-Win Workplace Toolkit

Access exclusive tools, templates, and resources featured in *The Win-Win Workplace* at TheWinWinWorkplace.com, including:

- *Inspiring Case Studies*
  (See how real companies are thriving in a Win-Win environment)
- *Win-Win Culture Assessment*
  (Evaluate your organization's alignment with thriving workplace practices)
- *Employee Ownership Blueprint*
  (A step-by-step guide to fostering a culture of ownership and collaboration)
- *Leadership Communication Templates*
  (Scripts and templates for engaging employees in meaningful conversations)
- *ROI Tracking Tool*
  (Measure the impact of employee-centered practices on your business)
- *Strategic Decision-Making Framework*
  (A practical guide for making decisions that benefit both employees and the bottom line)

- *Workplace Sustainability Checklist*

(Best practices for creating a sustainable, human-centered workplace culture)

Visit **TheWinWinWorkplace.com** or scan this QR code to explore these tools and start creating a workplace where everyone thrives!

About the Author

Angela Jackson, EdLD, has dedicated her life to eradicating the Zero-Sum way of working—with its inequity, alienation, and burnout—that shaped her childhood and, at the start of her career, almost killed her.

Now a nationally recognized thought leader on the future of work, Dr. Jackson traces her academic passion to her roots in a working-class family in North Chicago, IL. Raised by her grandparents, she tells audiences how work has always been front and center in her life. Her grandfather was a proud Chrysler assembly-line worker and union member. Her grandmother juggled part-time jobs—in a factory, as a maid, as a nurse's aide—to help provide for her granddaughter and the five foster children that the couple adopted over the years. "The biggest lessons I took from my grandparents," Dr. Jackson says, "were the value of empathy, the dignity in work, and how precarious financial security can be and how that impacts your life including your professional career."

The family's household balancing act fell apart after her grandmother was diagnosed with cancer and couldn't work. Five years later, the Chrysler plant shut down and her grandfather, at the age of 64, was laid off with all 5,500 of the factory's workforce.

"To this day, the heartbreak of our reality in those days sits at the forefront of my mind when I think about all the people who work full-time and still struggle," says Dr. Jackson.

"What kind of society are we if we accept that a full-time job isn't enough to support a full-time life?"

A scholarship to the University of Missouri-Columbia set her up to start searching for answers to that question. But not before a high-flying detour through corporate America. By the age of 30, she was a self-described workaholic making big money as the head of New Channels Marketing for Nokia, which paid for her to attend an Executive MBA program at INSEAD Business School. It was on a business trip for Nokia that Dr. Jackson, racing to a client meeting, crashed her car, landed in hospital, and changed her life.

Dr. Jackson went back to school, earning her doctorate in Education Leadership from Harvard and then setting out to address the thought that nagged at her throughout her long recovery from the car wreck: *There must be a better way to work, a better way to live.*

As a managing partner at the nonprofit New Profit, a venture philanthropy organization that supports breakthrough social entrepreneurs who are advancing equity and opportunity in America, Dr. Jackson led the firm's Future of Work Challenge. That initiative aimed to re-skill workers who were displaced by automation and the 2020–21 global COVID-19 pandemic, and prepare them for jobs with a growth trajectory.

Today, Dr. Jackson is the founder of Future Forward Strategies, a labor-market intelligence, design thinking, and strategy firm that assists leaders with transforming organizations and human capital infrastructure so that they can create positive impact—for their employees, their local communities and their environment—while maintaining competitiveness and improving their bottom lines. She has engaged with global business leaders from the likes of Walmart, Google, and JP Morgan Chase, and seen her research on an equitable future of work gain recognition in top-tier publications like *The Economist, Forbes, Harvard Business Review, Fortune, Fast Company*, and *Stanford Social Innovation Review.*

Dr. Jackson, a sought-after speaker on connecting social impact to business goals, is also a lecturer at Harvard University, where she teaches the next generation of students about leadership, entrepreneurship, and the future of work. While striving for a global new world order of work, Dr. Jackson practices what she preaches: Future Forward Strategies is a Win-Win workplace.

She and her husband and daughter divide their time between Brookline and New York City.

The Win-Win Workplace

 ## Share Your Win-Win Story!

The journey toward a workplace where employees and organizations thrive is one we're on together. Many of the case studies in this book came from people just like you. And with the next edition of *The Win-Win Workplace* in progress, I'd love to invite you to share your story!

Send me a story about a Win-Win workplace you've experienced or helped create. Whether it's a new initiative, a cultural shift, or a breakthrough that made a difference, your stories of success, challenges, and impact can inspire others.

Email me at **angela@thewinwinworkplace.com** with your story in **150 words or less.** We'll credit you in the next edition and celebrate the change you're helping to make!

Together, let's build workplaces where everyone wins.

Looking forward to hearing from you!
— Angela Jackson

Be Part of a Win-Win Movement!

Email ✉ **angela@thewinwinworkplace.com** with your story to inspire others and help reshape the future of work.

Dear reader,

Thank you for picking up this book and welcome to the worldwide BK community! You're joining a special group of people who have come together to create positive change in their lives, organizations, and communities.

What's BK all about?

Our mission is to connect people and ideas to create a world that works for all.

Why? Our communities, organizations, and lives get bogged down by old paradigms of self-interest, exclusion, hierarchy, and privilege. But we believe that can change. That's why we seek the leading experts on these challenges—and share their actionable ideas with you.

A welcome gift

To help you get started, we'd like to offer you a **free copy** of one of our bestselling ebooks:

bkconnection.com/welcome

When you claim your **free ebook**, you'll also be subscribed to our blog.

Our freshest insights

Access the best new tools and ideas for leaders at all levels on our blog at ideas.bkconnection.com.

Sincerely,

Your friends at Berrett-Koehler